THE WORKS OF SHAKESPEARE

EDITED FOR THE SYNDICS OF THE
CAMBRIDGE UNIVERSITY PRESS
BY
SIR ARTHUR QUILLER-COUCH
AND JOHN DOVER WILSON

THE TEMPEST

THE TEMPEST

CAMBRIDGE

AT THE UNIVERSITY PRESS

1969

PUBLISHED BY
THE SYNDICS OF THE CAMBRIDGE UNIVERSITY PRESS

Bentley House, 200 Euston Road, London, N.W. 1
American Branch: 32 East 57th Street, New York, N.Y. 10022

Standard Book Number:
521 07557 2 *clothbound*
521 09500 X *paperback*

First edition 1921
Reprinted 1939 1948 1957 1961 1965
First paperback edition 1969

*First printed in Great Britain at the University Press, Cambridge
Reprinted in Great Britain by Hazell Watson & Viney Ltd,
Aylesbury, Bucks*

CONTENTS

CONTENTS

GENERAL INTRODUCTION

I

Editions of Shakespeare multiply; but it is now many years since the last attempt was made at a complete recension of Shakespeare's text, based upon a study and comparison, line by line, of the existing materials. In the interval scholars have made many discoveries, and not a few worthy to be called illuminating; since the new light they shed on these materials exhibits them (as we believe) in truer proportions with truer relative values.

We shall indicate, by and by, the most important of these discoveries, as justifying a belief that since the day, some three hundred years ago, when preparations were begun in the printing-house of William Jaggard and his son Isaac for the issue of the First Folio, no moment has been more favourable for auspicating a text of the plays and poems than that which begets the occasion of this new one. But no time must be lost in assuring the reader that we enter upon our task diffidently, with a sense of high adventure tempered by a consciousness of grave responsibility; and that at the outset we have chosen for phylactery these wise words by one of Shakespeare's wisest editors, William Aldis Wright—'After a considerable experience I feel justified in saying that in most cases ignorance and conceit are the fruitful parents of conjectural emendation.' To have done with excuses, we desire lastly that the reader will not take offence at this or that which seems at first sight an innovation upon the 'Shakespeares' to which he is accustomed: that he will refrain at any rate from condemning us before making sure that we are not cutting Shakespeare free from the accretions of a long line of editors.

II

But we have designed these volumes also for the pocket of the ordinary lover of Shakespeare, because time alters the catholic approach to him, if by insensible degrees, no less thoroughly than it deflects that of the esoteric student. 'What mankind have long possessed they have often examined and compared: and if they persist to value the possession, it is because frequent comparisons have confirmed opinion in its favour.' So wrote Samuel Johnson in the Preface to his edition of the Plays of Shakespeare, published in 1765; adding that these plays have 'passed through variations of taste and changes of manners, and, as they devolved from one generation to another, have received new honours at every transmission....The sand heaped by one flood is scattered by another, but the rock always continues in its place. The stream of Time, which is continually washing the dissoluble fabricks of other poets, passes without injury by the adamant of *Shakespeare*.'

'In the fine arts'—writes a later critic, Professor Barrett Wendell, also of Shakespeare—'a man of genius is he who in perception and in expression alike, in thought and in phrase, instinctively so does his work that his work remains significant after the conditions in which he actually produced it are past. The work of any man of genius, then, is susceptible of endless comment and interpretation, varying as the generations of posterity vary from his and from one another.'

Thus, in the eighteenth and nineteenth centuries, two critics among many have echoed the line which Ben Jonson penned for the First Folio of 1623, prescient and yet (one may assert) not fully awake to his own prescience

He was not of an age, but for all time!

For, obscure and mostly insignificant as are the collected details of Shakespeare's life and career, the vicissitudes of his reputation have never lacked evidence from the first, and in later times have rather suffered from a cloud of witness. In the beginning, having come up from Stratford-on-Avon to London (about 1586) to try his fortune, this youth managed to open the back door of Burbage's Theatre and gain employment as an actor. Burbage must soon have set him the additional task of furbishing and 'bumbasting out' old plays for revival—with results at which the original authors very naturally took offence: for as early as 1592 Robert Greene utters (from his death-bed) his famous invective upon our young man as 'an upstart Crow beautified with our feathers'; warning his literary fellow-playwrights, 'it is pittee men of such rare wits should be subject to the pleasures of such rude groomes.' Greene's contemptuous language may pass. Its vehement anger pretty plainly proves that, even so early, our dramatic apprentice had learnt to make himself formidable.

We may start from the previous year 1591, and take the ensuing twenty as the period covering Shakespeare's career as a dramatist. Did his fame grow as nowadays in retrospect we can see his poetical power maturing from *Love's Labour's Lost* up to *King Lear* and on to *The Tempest*? The little contemporary evidence is curious, and tells us at once that it did and that it did not. For example in 1598 we have Francis Meres, a learned graduate of Cambridge, asserting that 'among the English he is the most excellent in both kinds [Tragedy and Comedy] for the Stage,' rivalling the fame of Seneca in the one kind and of Plautus in the other. As against this we find, at the same date and in Meres' University, the authors of *The Pilgrimage to Parnassus* attempting more than one laugh at him as belonging to a tribe of playwrights fashionable but unlettered. Vaguely, yet with some certainty, the early Elizabethan dramatists fall for us into two opponent camps; the University wits and 'literary' tribesmen coming to

recognise (or being bullied into recognising) Ben Jonson
for their champion, while Shakespeare almost at unawares
grows to his stature as chief challenger on behalf of the
theatre-men who worked for the stage and its daily
bread, with no hankering side-glance after the honours
and diuturnity of print. His election to this eminence
is nowhere, in so many words, asserted. When the two
parties became publicly and violently embroiled in the
wordy stage-war—which started between Jonson on the
one side and Dekker and Marston on the other, and
lasted from 1599 to 1602—he neither lent his name to the
battle nor apparently deigned to participate in it. As
we interpret the story, he could not help being intel-
lectually head-and-shoulders above all who made his
party: but he enjoyed no quarrel, and was, in fact, by
nature too generously indolent, and withal too modest,
and yet again too busy with his work, to worry himself
with contention. Gentle and 'sweet' (his own favourite
word), or some equivalent for these, are steady epithets
of all who knew him or had heard his contemporaries
talk about him. *De forti dulcedo*—'a handsome well-
shaped man' Aubrey tells us of report; 'very good company and of a readie and pleasant smooth witt.' There
is no evidence at all that he set an exorbitant price on
himself: rather, out of silence and contrast, we get a
cumulative impression that he claimed a most modest
one. There are hints enough that the generation for
which he worked recognised him for a man of parts and
promise; but again out of silence and contrast we in-
sensibly gather the conviction that it never occurred to
his fellows to regard him as a mountainous man, 'out-
topping knowledge'; and that he himself, could he have
foreseen Matthew Arnold's famous sonnet, would have
found in it a modest gratification combined with something like amazement. His death (in middle age) pro-
voked no such general outburst of lamentation as Sidney's
did; his life no such running fire of detraction as did

Jonson's. He retired and died, moderately well-to-do, in the country town of his birth. The copyright (as we call it) of his plays belonged to the theatre or Company for which they were written: and he never troubled himself or anybody to collect, correct, and print them. They were first gathered and given to the world by two fellow-actors, John Heminge and Henry Condell, late in 1623, or more than seven-and-a-half years after his death.

Again we must not make too much of this: for one only of the Elizabethan dramatists had hitherto sought what fame might come of printing his plays for a secondary judgment by the reader; and not one in Shakespeare's life-time. The exception of course was Ben Jonson, who in 1616 had brought together and issued nine pieces in a folio volume.

Some may argue that between the date of his death and that of the First Folio of 1623 Shakespeare's fame had vastly grown, ·quoting Jonson's splendid and expressly written encomium which follows the Folio Preface, with its allusion to Basse's elegy lamenting that our 'rare Tragedian' had not been laid to rest beside Chaucer and Spenser and Beaumont in Westminster Abbey:

> Renownéd Spenser lye a thought more nye
> To learnéd Chaucer, and rare Beaumont lye
> A little neerer Spenser, to make roome
> For Shakespeare in your threefold, fowerfold Tombe.
> To lodge all fowre in one bed make a shift
> Vntill Doomesdaye, for hardly will a fift
> Betwixt y^s day and y^t by Fate be slayne
> For whom your Curtaines may be drawn againe...

upon which Jonson retorts in apostrophe:

> My Shakespeare, rise; I will not lodge thee by
> Chaucer or Spenser, or bid Beaumont lye
> A little further, to make thee a roome...
> Thou art a Moniment, without a tombe,
> And art alive still, while thy Booke doth live,
> And we have wits to read, and praise to give.

But dedicatory verse in that age had a proper and recognised pitch: and if a reader in 1623 found the praise not extravagant, as we find it not extravagant to-day, his reason for it and ours would be different. It seems safer to turn for Jonson's real opinion to the famous passage in *Timber or Discoveries*, frank as it is and familiarly spoken, with its confession that he 'loved the man' and its characteristic glance at 'the players' (Heminge and Condell) for their praise of Shakespeare's facility:

His mind and hand went together: And what he thought he uttered with that easiness that wee have scarce received from him a blot on his papers.

Upon this Jonson retorts vivaciously but with some justice:

I remember, the Players have often mentioned it as an honour to Shakespeare that in his writing (whatsoever he penn'd) hee never blotted out line. My answer hath beene, would he have blotted a thousand, which they thought a malevolent speech. I had not told posterity this, but for their ignorance, who chose that circumstance to commend their friend by, wherein he most faulted...

III

Milton's

What needs my Shakespeare for his honour'd Bones

was prefixed anonymously to the Second Folio of 1632; and he, too, while praising the 'unvalu'd Book' for its 'Delphick lines,' dwells on Shakespeare's easiness:

For whilst to th' shame of slow-endeavouring art
Thy easie numbers flow...

Shakespeare, in sum, is still a warbler of 'native Woodnotes wilde,' and yet already a Book, or in process of becoming one. He was a book to Suckling (*ob.* 1641, aged thirty-two) who 'supplemented' a passage from *Lucrece*, and had his own portrait painted by Vandyke with a copy of the First Folio under his hand, open at the play of *Hamlet*. He was a book, again, to King Charles I, whose copy of the Second Folio (still preserved at Windsor) may be the one that went with him in his last distressful wanderings and was, as Milton tells us in *Eikonoklastes*, 'the Closet Companion of these his solitudes.' By this time, indeed, Shakespeare had become a book perforce—a book or nothing—through the closing of the theatres in 1642, and a book he remains for eighteen years or so.

With the Restoration the theatres re-open and he starts up at once again as a playwright in favour and sufficiently alive to be bandied between fervent admiration and nonchalant acceptance. Samuel Pepys goes to the theatre and notes that *Macbeth* is 'a pretty good play' (but he comes to 'like it mightily,' 'a most excellent play in all respects, but especially in divertisement though it be a deep tragedy; which is a strange perfection in a tragedy, it being most proper here and suitable'). *Romeo and Juliet* is 'a play of itself the worst I ever saw in my life,' *The Midsummer-Night's Dream* 'a most insipid ridiculous play,' and *Twelfth Night* 'but a silly play,' 'one of the weakest plays I ever saw on the stage.'

1660, August 20.—To Deptford by water reading *Othello, Moore of Venice*, which I ever heretofore esteemed a mighty good play, but having so lately read *The Adventures of Five Houres*, it seems a mean thing.

But *Hamlet* conquers him, and he witnesses four performances by Betterton with a rising rapture.

Yet Dryden, although he will play any conceivable trick in 'adapting'—witness *All for Love* and his misdeed, with D'Avenant's aid, upon *The Tempest*—never speaks of Shakespeare but as a classic. In practice Shakespeare is so little sacrosanct to him that to except him from any verdict passed on Cibber and Garrick for their impertinences in a later age would be hypocrisy—the homage paid by cowardice to a great name. But when he talks as a critic, his voice never falters. 'Shakespeare's sacred name,' 'Shakespeare, who many times has written better than any poet,' 'the poet Æschylus was held in the same veneration by the Athenians of after ages as Shakespeare is by us'—*that* is Dryden's way of talking. Here, in a sentence, is his manly apology:

Therefore let not Shakespear suffer for our sakes: 'tis our fault, who succeed him in an Age which is more refin'd, if we imitate him so ill that we copy his failings only and make a virtue of that in our Writings which in his was an imperfection,

and here, in another, is his summary:

Shakespear had a Universal mind, which comprehended all Characters and Passions.

IV

With Nicholas Rowe, the first general editor (1709), we open the second period of Shakespeare's progress towards canonisation. We may call it as we list the Eighteenth Century period or the period of criticism and conjectural emendation, in both of which arts, within somewhat strict limits, our Eighteenth Century men excelled. Their criticism walked within a narrow and formal conception of the poetic art—or, we may say, a fixed idea of it to which the loose magnificence of Shakespeare was naturally abhorrent. Pope (1725) finds him (as Matthew Arnold[1] found him in a later age) a sad sinner against art, and we may see the alternate fascination and repulsion which agitated Pope reproduced in long exaggerating shadows across the evidence of Voltaire; who during his sojourn in England (1726–9) read Shakespeare voraciously, to imitate him sedulously; and went home to preach Shakespeare to Europe: until conscience constrained him to denounce the man for a buffoon and his

[1] 'He is the richest, the most powerful, the most delightful of poets: he is not altogether, nor even eminently, an artist'—*Mixed Essays*.

works for a vast and horrible dunghill in which the Gallic cock might perchance happen on some few pearls.

For their conjectural emendation these men of the Eighteenth Century had not only the nice aptitude of a close literary set nurtured upon the Greek and Latin Classics: but, to play with, a text admittedly corrupt and calling aloud for improvement—considered as belonging to a semi-barbarous age, and so as material upon which any polite taste had free licence to improve: a text, moreover, upon which the tradition of scholarship as yet enjoined no meticulous research. Roughly speaking, any scholar of the Eighteenth Century was acquitted if he familiarised himself with one or another of the Folio versions and restored any doubtful passage 'out of his own head.' The marvels they accomplished by this simple process remain an enormous credit to them and no less a wonder to us: and, in particular, no editor should pass Lewis Theobald without a salute—' *splendid-emendax.*' Upon Theobald follow Hanmer (1743–4)— a polite country gentleman, retired from the Speaker-ship of the House of Commons and enjoying his leisure, Bishop Warburton (1747), Doctor Johnson (whose eight volumes, after long gestation, came to birth in 1765), Capell (1768), Steevens (1766 and 1773), the indefatigable Malone (1790), Isaac Reed, editor of the First Variorum, published in twenty-one volumes in 1803. Thus, starting from Rowe, we cover a fair hundred years in the course of which we may fairly say, conjectural criticism did all it could upon its knowledge— with the qualification, perhaps, that our author never tempted Bentley to delight mankind by improving his poetry.

But when a poet is acknowledged to be pre-eminent by such a succession of the first class as Dryden, Pope and Samuel Johnson, his throne as a classic is secure, and doubly secure because Dryden, Pope and Johnson, all differently and all in turn, belonged to an age which had to acknowledge his greatness against all prejudice of more or less rigid rule.

V

So we pass to a third stage when, with all this curious guesswork heaped upon Shakespeare's text and all this tribute superimposed by the greatest critics of a reluctant age, the Romantics lay hold on him and exalt him for a demigod. Coleridge, Schlegel, Hazlitt, Lamb take their turn (Swinburne belatedly continuing the tradition up to yesterday), and all—but Coleridge most of all—have wonderful interpretations to give us. The mischief is not only that Shakespeare becomes a sort of national idol against whom a man can offer no criticism save timidly (as one standing between a lion and a unicorn), but that every second-rate or third-rate 'Elizabethan' with a grip on Shakespeare's skirt is lifted to a place beside him; with the result that Shakespeare loses his right eminence above his contemporaries, while his age enjoys above the seventeenth and eighteenth centuries an exaltation which the sober mind cannot accept as just. Moreover in the intervals of over-estimating, we make these contemporaries Shakespeare's whipping-boys. We cannot accept the plain fact that Shakespeare had often to do odd jobs, was often careless, and sometimes wrote extremely ill. As W. E. Henley put it:

Our worship must have for its object something flawless, something utterly without spot or blemish. We can be satisfied with nothing less than an entire and perfect chrysolite, and we cannot taste our Shakespeare at his worst without a longing to father his faults upon somebody else—Marlowe, for instance, or Greene or Fletcher—and a fury of proving, that our divinity was incapable of them.

Through the nineteenth century, and even to this day, the volume of laudation swells and rises, ever with a German guttural increasing in self-assertion at the back of the uproar; until many an honest fellow, conscious of loving letters in a plain way, must surely long for the steadying accent of someone who can keep his head in the tumult; not, perhaps, for another Johnson, but at least for an outspoken utterance on the lines of Johnson's famous Preface, which Adam Smith styled 'the most manly piece of criticism that was ever published in any country.' Surely, as Ben Jonson laughed at Shakespeare for saying it of Caesar, it is high time we laughed at those who keep saying of Shakespeare that he 'did never wrong but with just cause.' Few, in Plato's phrase, are the initiate, many the thyrsus-bearers; and the effect of the Shakespearian thyrsus upon a crowd of its carriers would seem to be quite peculiarly intoxicant. It has been computed that of the lunatics at present under ward or at large in the British Isles, a good third suffer from religious mania, a fifth from a delusion that they belong to the Royal Family, while another fifth believe either that they *are* Shakespeare, or that they are the friends or relatives or champions of somebody else, whose clothes and reputation 'that Stratford clown' managed to steal; or, anyhow, that Shakespeare did anything imaginable but unlikely, from touching up the Authorised Version to practising as a veterinary surgeon.

Yet these extravagances deserve pity rather than laughter: for what they reveal is but the unbalanced side of a very human and not ignoble craving. We cannot help wanting to know more of the *man* who has befriended our lives so constantly, so sunnily; to whom we have owed so many spirited incentives of our childhood—'enrichers of the fancy'—in Charles Lamb's phrase:

Strengtheners of virtue, a withdrawing from all selfish and mercenary thoughts, a lesson of all sweet and honourable thoughts and actions, to teach you courtesy, benignity, generosity, humanity...

with whose sword at hip we have walked lovers' path;

to whom we have resorted so confidently in dark or in solitary hours.

Doubtless it were a counsel of perfection to accept his works gratefully and let the man go. Doubtless that word should be enough for us in which Homer said farewell to the Delian maidens—'Good-bye, my dears: and hereafter, should any traveller happen along and ask you "Who was the sweetest singer ever landed on your beach?" make answer to him civilly—"Sir, he was just a blind man, and his home (he said) in steep Chios."'

Doubtless, we say, it were a counsel of perfection to accept the writings of Shakespeare even so simply, so gratefully, and to let the man go. But he has meant so much to us! We resent the idea of him as 'out-topping knowledge' derisive of our 'foiled searchings.' We demand, as Jacob, after wrestling all night with the angel, demanded:

Tell me, I pray thee, thy name. And the man answered, Wherefore is it that thou askest my name? And he blessed him and departed.

But out of the cumulative labour of nineteenth century students innumerable to tell—all devoted, all persistent, the most of them with scarcely a critical gift beyond patience and arithmetic (but we must except Collier, Gervinus, Delius, Furnivall, and the Cambridge editors)—arose among them, as an atoll grows out of Ocean, by infinite verse-countings and other tests, that century's great discovery—of the chronological order in which Shakespeare wrote his plays.

VI

Now the one priceless and irrefragable boon of this discovery is the steady light it throws upon Shakespeare's development as an artist: with its pauses, breaks, trybacks, hesitations, advances, explain them how we may. But also, and less legitimately, it flatters the curiosity of those who want to know about the man and his private life by persuading them that from the Plays and the Sonnets—but especially the Sonnets—thus set out in right chronological order, can be expressed a continuous and even a detailed biography.

There seems no good reason why scholars and men of letters should decry one another's work just because the ways of it differ. All our roads may lead to Shakespeare in the end. Yet we may protest, or at least enter a warning, that personal gossip based on nothing more secure than internal evidence interpreted through a critic's own proclivities of belief, may easily stray through excess into impertinence. When, for example, we are told that 'every one who has read Shakespeare's works with any care must admit that Shakespeare was a snob of the purest English water,' and find that, apart from the ascertained fact of his father's having applied more than once, and at length with success, to Herald's College for a coat of arms, the evidence consists in little more than assertions that 'aristocratic tastes were natural to him: inherent indeed in the delicate sensitiveness of his beauty-loving temperament' and that 'in all his writings he praises lords and gentlemen and runs down the common people,' we cannot help telling ourselves that it may be so indeed, or again it may not, but we require more assurance than this before constructing or taking away any man's character, be he living or dead. Nor is the argument reinforced by bidding us count and note the proportion of kings, lords and men of title in Shakespeare's *dramatis personae*: since in the first place almost all the Elizabethan playwrights have a similar preference for grandees, and this (apart from the actors' liking to be seen and the public's liking to see them, in fine raiment) for the simple economic reason that the theatrical wardrobes of that time held a limited stock of expensive costumes: and secondly because (in writing their tragedies at any rate) these playwrights know by instinct what Aristotle had long ago pointed out from induction—that your

tragic hero on the stage should preferably be a person
of high worldly estate; and this again for several reasons
but chiefly for the elementary one that the higher the
eminence from which a man falls the harder he hits the
ground—and our imagination. When, above Dover cliff,
blind Gloucester turns to the accent of old demented
Lear:

> The trick of that voice I do well remember:
> Is't not the King?

And Lear catches himself up to answer:

> Ay, every inch a king!

When Wolsey gets his soul ready to fall like Lucifer:

> I have touched the highest point of all my greatness;
> And from that full meridian of my glory,
> I haste now to my setting: I shall fall
> Like a bright exhalation in the evening,
> And no man see me more.

When 'royal Egypt' lifts the dirge over Antony, who,
but for her, were living and held the sceptre of the
world:

> O, withered is the garland of the war,
> The soldier's pole is fallen: young boys and girls
> Are level now with men; the odds is gone,
> And there is nothing left remarkable
> Beneath the visiting moon—

are we to believe it was by snobbery—by the worship of
eminence for that which true eminence disdains—that
Shakespeare crawled into the hearts of princes and
governors? that he learned this so grand utterance
through servility, to reproduce it by a trick?

VII

We should be cautious, too, in listening to those
who, all so variously, utilise the Sonnets to construct
fancy histories of Shakespeare's personal life and actual
experiences. Most of us, at one time or another, have

played with these guesses more or less seriously, and must admit their fascination. Even when they draw us close to abhorrent ground we feel like the man in Plato, who coming near the city wall, saw in the distance the corpses of certain malefactors laid without it and, after a long time fighting between unholy temptation and decent repulsion, yielding at length, ran towards the carrion prizing his eyes wide and crying 'Feed your fill, you wretches!' We must admit, too, how much of insight some casual, recovered touch (as it were) of the real man's hand may give. Moreover who can doubt that every true man, small or great, leaves some print of himself on his work, or indeed that he *must* if his work be literature, which is so personal a thing. As Sir Walter Raleigh puts it, 'No man can walk abroad save on his own shadow.' Yes, but as another writer, Mr Morton Luce, well comments 'an author may be—perhaps ought to be—something inferior to his work.'

We may make yet one more admission. The most of us are to some degree potential poets, but have not the gift to express ourselves. When a great poet happens along, his work, as Johnson said of Gray's *Elegy* 'abounds with images which find a mirror in every mind, and with sentiments to which every heart returns an echo.' Benedetto Croce would tell us that this power of genius over the aesthetic in ordinary man—over you or me—is quantitative, is but a matter of degree. But whether we consent with Croce or insist that the difference is a difference of quality, it remains a fact that while the poet, being human, is undoubtedly shaped by such joys and woes as befal you and me, and Cluvienus, their effect on him may be as wayward as human intelligence can conceive, and that therefore it is mere guesswork to say that, because Shakespeare writes this or that in *Lear* or in the Sonnets, therefore this or that must have happened in his private life to account for his writing *just so.*

T.T.—2

VIII

But—to hark back—surely the true use to which we should put the grand discovery of our fathers in the last century—the right chronological order of the Plays—is to trace his development as an artist rather than to hunt down the man who enjoined to be written over his grave:

> Good friend, for Jesus sake forbear...

For many another man has come to sorrow before now over a dark lady, as many another has owned a second-best bed; but only one man has progressed from *Love's Labour's Lost*, on to *As You Like It*, to *Twelfth Night*; only one has proceeded from these comedies to *Hamlet*, *Othello*, *Lear*, *Antony and Cleopatra*; only one has filled up the intervals with *Henry IV*, Parts·i and ii, with *Julius Caesar*, with *Coriolanus*; only one, in years of physical weakness, has imagined for us an Imogen; only one has closed upon the woven magic of *The Tempest*. It may be asked, and reasonably, Why, believing the discovery of the true chronological order to be so important, we have not arranged our edition in accordance with it? To this we answer simply that the old arrangement has an historical value and some consecration of ancient sentiment, with neither of which we thought it worth while to interfere, seeing that a chronological list, occupying but a page or so, will serve the purpose more handily; and, for the rest, the original date of each separate play is almost impossible to fix: so many of them being, as they have reached us, revisions of revisions. Our prefatory notes will *attempt* to assign its date to each play. But here is a tentative inventory:

Before 1595 Henry VI (other men's work, revised).
Richard III (part only).
Titus Andronicus (a few touches only).
The Comedy of Errors.
The Two Gentlemen of Verona.

Venus and Adonis (1593).
The Rape of Lucrece (1594).
?Sonnets (begun).
1595–1597 Love's Labour's Lost (final form).
?All's Well That Ends Well (first form).
A Midsummer-Night's Dream.
Romeo and Juliet.
King John.
The Taming of the Shrew (?part only).
Richard II.
The Merchant of Venice.
1598–1600 Henry IV. Part I.
Henry IV. Part II.
The Merry Wives of Windsor (?part only).
Much Ado About Nothing.
Henry V (?final form).
As You Like It.
Twelfth Night.
Julius Caesar.
1601–1604 Hamlet.
Troilus and Cressida.
All's Well That Ends Well (final form).
Measure for Measure.
Othello.
1605–1608 Macbeth.
King Lear.
Antony and Cleopatra.
Timon of Athens (part only).
Coriolanus.
Pericles (part only).
1609–1613 Cymbeline.
The Winter's Tale.
The Tempest.
Henry VIII (part only).

Although, for reasons given, the dates of several plays
in their earliest form cannot yet, and may never, be finally
determined, the above list gives a rough chronological
order of the final forms in which we have received them.
It claims to no more: but this much is, so far as it
goes, invaluable. For if, as our younger critics hold,
almost with one accord, the true business of criticism be

to interpret and elucidate for other men an artist's 'expression,' this compass of the last century's invention should guide them to many new discoveries. Helped by yet later inventions (to be discussed in the second part of this Introduction) it may carry them across seas hitherto uncharted. Even by itself it gives us invaluable guidance in tracing Shakespeare's development as a playwright and a poet; which is surely better worth our while than speculation on his private affairs.

As we join the words 'playwright' and 'poet,' our memory connects two stray sentences overheard at different times in the theatre—a man's voice muttering between the third and fourth Acts of *Hamlet*, 'And he turned off plays like this, while he was going, at the rate of two a year!'—and the voice of an artless maiden in the stalls, responsive to Juliet's passion: 'I do like Shakespeare, don't you? He has such a way of putting things!'

IX

A wise reader will constantly remember that Shakespeare was an indefatigable playwright, and find endless reward of curiosity in tracing the experiments by which he learned to master the craft of the stage. Nevertheless to consider Shakespeare primarily as a playwright, and to contend that his verse should be treated on the stage as 'material for an actor to juggle with and use to the best advantage of the drama' is to miss Shakespeare's true stature altogether. We hope, indeed, that our text will make him more intelligible theatrically in not a few places. For a single example—the Folio prints *Romeo and Juliet* straight through without break of Act or Scene. If we turn to any modern edition, at the beginning of Act II we shall find two scenes: the one placed in a lane outside Capulet's orchard, the other within the orchard overlooked by Juliet's balcony: and this second

scene opens with *Enter Romeo*, and with Romeo's remark
'He jests at scars that never felt a wound'—quite as if
he had barked his shins in climbing over the wall, and
his romantic amorous ardour was making nothing of it.
But we have only to read carefully to convince ourselves
that these two scenes are one scene: that the lane and
its wall should come just athwart one corner of the stage:
that Romeo, having climbed the wall, crouches close,
listening, and laughing to himself while he overhears his
baffled comrades discussing him; and that when they
give up the chase and their footsteps die away, it is as
instant comment upon Mercutio's loose cynical talk about
love, King Cophetua, 'poperin pears,' etc., that he
dismisses it with:

He (*scilicet* Mercutio) jests at scars that never felt a wound

and so turns to the light breaking from Juliet's window.
In all the standard texts the line is pointless.

This for a specimen. We must ever bear in mind that
Shakespeare wrote for the stage: but men's eyes nowadays
read his page a thousand times for any once they see it
enacted. It were a feeble compliment to-day to call
him merely our 'great national Playwright.' He is that:
but he is much more—he is very much more—he is more
by difference of quality. He is our great national Poet.

X

By keeping—as with fair ease we can—a mental list
of the plays in their right chronological order—we can
trace the Poet as he attains mastery through opera-
tion. We watch the young experimenter in *Venus and
Adonis* at play with words, intent on the game of
elaborate phrase-making as ever kitten was intent on
chasing her own tail. We note, even so early, an
extraordinary gift of concreteness—of translating idea
into visible images—which comes naturally to him and

differentiates him from his elders and compeers—from
Marlowe for instance:

> Upon this promise did he raise his chin
> Like a dive-dipper peering through a wave
> Which, being look'd on, ducks as quickly in...

> Lo! here the gentle lark, weary of rest,
> From his moist cabinet mounts up on high...

> Or, as the snail, whose tender horns being hit,
> Shrinks backward in his shelly cave with pain...

We trace up this word-play through such lines as

> The singing masons building roofs of gold,

and

> Still quiring to the young-eyed cherubins,

to the commanding style of

> Sleep that knits up the ravelled sleeve of care

or of

>   Men must endure
> Their going hence even as their coming hither,
> Ripeness is all—

and from command to tyranny: until—in *Antony and
Cleopatra* for example—nouns scurry to do the work of
verbs, adverbs and adjectives form fours, sentences sweat
and groan like porters with three thoughts piled on one
back, and not one dares mutiny any more than Ariel
dares it against Prospero's most delicate bidding. Prospero
himself, in his narrative of how he reached the island,
throws all grammar to the winds, as does Imogen in
her panting haste to find Milford Haven. Shakespeare in
fine, and at the utmost of his quality, sinks all grammar
in the heave and swell of speech under emotion. And in
the end we are left to question, How did this man learn
to make sentences mean so much more than they say?
how contrive his voice so that four quite simple words,
'Think, we had mothers!' or 'The rest is silence' chime
with overtones and undertones that so deepen all the
space and meaning of life between hell and heaven?

XI

Concurrently we watch him a craftsman busy on the day's work, tinkering upon old plays, old chronicles, other men's romances; borrowing other men's inventions, not in the least scrupulous over pillaging his own; learning to take any ordinary page of North's Plutarch or of Holinshed and transmute it, by just a frugal touch, into gold; in his later years essaying about the hardest technical difficulty a dramatist can propose to himself, and, beaten thrice—in *Pericles*, in *Cymbeline*, in *The Winter's Tale*—with a fourth and last shot, in *The Tempest* bringing down his quarry from the sky.

And meanwhile he is creating Falstaff and Mistress Quickly; Hamlet, Iago, Lear and Lear's fool; Rosalind and Imogen and Cleopatra; with the moonshine of *A Midsummer-Night's Dream*, the mirk of *Macbeth*, the scents of Juliet's garden, the frozen platform of Elsinore, the rainbow surf of Prospero's island; and above all interpreting, for refreshment of heart and mind, that miracle of miracles—his native England in early summer.

An editor, engaged to clear the text of such a poet should be as happily devout as young Ion sweeping out the shrine of Apollo himself.

Q.

TEXTUAL INTRODUCTION

Within this last decade the study of Shakespearian texts has been given a new trend by three distinct though closely related discoveries.

The first is that of Mr A. W. Pollard, originator of a new scientific method—critical Shakespearian bibliography. In a series of works (*Shakespeare Folios and Quartos*, 1909; *King Richard II, a New Quarto*, 1916; *Shakespeare's Fight with the Pirates*, 1917, etc.) Mr Pollard has demonstrated that dramatic MSS which reached the printer's hands in Shakespeare's day were generally theatrical prompt-copy; that many of these are likely to have been in the author's autograph; and that, therefore, the first editions of Shakespeare's plays—the quartos in particular—possess a much higher authority than editors have hitherto been inclined to allow them.

The second discovery, originally made by Mr Percy Simpson (*Shakespearian Punctuation*, 1911), though since developed by Mr Pollard, affects the vitally important question of the stops in the Folio and Quartos, which are now seen to be not the haphazard peppering of ignorant compositors, as all previous editors have regarded them, but play-house punctuation, directing the actors how to speak their lines.

The third and most sensational discovery of all came to light in 1916, when Sir Edward Maunde Thompson boldly claimed, in his *Shakespeare's Handwriting*, that one of several hands found in the confused and partially revised manuscript play *Sir Thomas More*, now in the British Museum, was that of Shakespeare himself, and that therefore we now have three pages of authentic Shakespearian 'copy' in our possession. Not all scholars are as yet prepared to accept this ascription unreservedly: but none question Sir Edward Maunde Thompson's thesis that these three pages are written in a hand of at least the same class as that seen in the six Shakespearian signatures; and this is enough to make the 'Shakespearian' addition to *Sir Thomas More* an instrument of the highest value for an editor of Shakespeare.

In short we believe that we know how Shakespeare wrote; we have a definite clue to his system of punctuation; we feel confident that often nothing but a compositor stands between us and the original manuscript; we can at times even creep into the compositor's skin and catch glimpses of the manuscript through his eyes. The door of Shakespeare's workshop stands ajar.

1. *Classification and Selection of Texts.*

A modern editor of Shakespeare has to reckon with three distinct groups of textual material. First in importance comes the Folio of 1623. Save for a haphazard set of reprints of nine plays, by or attributed to Shakespeare, brought together without any general title-page in 1619, this is the earliest collected edition of Shakespeare's works and includes all the plays now in the canon except *Pericles*, which was added in the third Folio (1664). A number of plays, however, had seen light, as individual publications, before the First Folio appeared, and Mr Pollard has provisionally sorted out these Quartos, as they are called, into two species: the 'good' and the 'bad.' The Good Quartos form our second group of textual material, and are fourteen in number, viz.:

Titus Andronicus	1594
Richard II	1597
Richard III	1597
Love's Labour's Lost	1598
Henry IV i	1598
Romeo and Juliet	1599
Merchant of Venice	1600
Much Ado about Nothing	1600
Henry IV ii	1600
Midsummer-Night's Dream	1600

Hamlet	1604–5
Lear	1608
Troilus and Cressida	1609
Othello	1622

To these may be added *Venus and Adonis* (1593), *The Rape of Lucrece* (1594) and the *Sonnets* (1609), thus bringing the number up to seventeen. They are called Good Quartos because they give us on the whole 'good' texts, which often formed the basis for the corresponding texts of the Folio. They possess, moreover, the hall-mark of respectability, inasmuch as all but two were regularly entered, previous to publication, in the Stationers' Register, and such entries carry with them the presumption that the printer came by his 'copy' in the honest way of business. The two exceptions (*Love's Labour's Lost* and *Romeo and Juliet*) are more apparent than real; since here the absence of entry may be explained by the fact that a 'bad' text had already been issued, though only one of the 'bad' texts has survived as evidence. The mention of 'bad' texts introduces us to the third group, a small one of five plays, known as the Bad Quartos, none of which was regularly entered in the Stationers' Register before publication, a circumstance suspicious in itself and made more so by the patent imperfections of the texts they present. They comprise:

Romeo and Juliet	1597
Henry V	1600
Merry Wives	1602
Hamlet	1603
Pericles	1608

The current explanation of the first four of these texts is that they were based upon theatrical abridgments of full-length manuscripts, partially revised by Shakespeare, and were touched up for publication by a pirate-actor who played in the completely revised versions.

With the exception of *Richard II* (1608), which contained for the first time the previously excluded Parliament Scene, and perhaps of *Othello* (1630), the foregoing texts are all with which an editor of Shakespeare need seriously concern himself, since other Folios and Quartos are simply reprints, for the production of which it is highly improbable that the printers had recourse to any manuscript authority. Variant readings, therefore, in later Folios and in Quarto-reprints can claim no recognition beyond that due to the guess of a more or less intelligent compositor or printer's reader. As the work of craftsmen accustomed to proof-reading in Shakespeare's day, they are of interest; but they should be accepted with the greatest caution.

An editor's first business is to select his text. With plays which only appear in the Folio, he has of course no alternative. Nor is the choice difficult when there exists a Bad Quarto version of a Folio play; for the Folio here obviously claims priority, though where the Bad Quarto presents variant readings, strongly suggestive of Shakespeare, they should be considered, and, provided good reason can be shown, may even be accepted. The task, however, is more ticklish when both Folio and Good Quarto versions exist. Here we have to reckon with the possibility that the Good Quarto was printed direct from Shakespeare's autograph copy; and, in any event, where the Folio text, as often happens, is demonstrably derived from a late edition of the Quarto, it is clearly necessary to go back to the *editio princeps* of that Quarto, which brings one into the closest proximity now possible with the manuscript of the author. The real difficulty arises when the Folio and Good Quarto texts differ in such a way as to suggest that they are taken from different manuscript sources. Then the editor has to decide, if he can, which of the two sources is the more authoritative. Such a decision involves a preliminary bibliographical analysis of the printed texts, to define the character of the printer's 'copy.'

2. *Definition of the 'Copy.'*

The 'copy' is the manuscript (or book) delivered to the printer and used by the compositor in setting up the lines of type. It is, as we shall see, highly important for an editor constantly to bear the compositor in mind. It is still more important to realise the nature of the particular 'copy' which the compositor has before his eyes in setting up the text. Now most dramatic manuscripts which reached the printing-houses in Shakespeare's time were of play-house origin. Probably they would be prompt-copies; and prompt-copy might be of two kinds: author's manuscript or a transcript of it. But a play would seldom be transcribed in full for an acting company, since this would cost time and money and increase the risk of piracy. The idea that our printed texts are separated from the author's original by an indefinite series of intervening transcripts, an idea which has haunted editors from Dr Johnson's day to this, may therefore be dismissed. The chances are that it was prompt-copy which came to the printer's hand, and that often the prompt-copy was, as the First Folio puts it, the 'true original.'

It must be remembered, however, that prompt-copy was subject to many chances and changes. The author is perhaps working over an old play, and his reconstruction may here and there be careless. The play when drafted became the property of the company, and they were free to make what alterations they chose. When it came to 'plotting' the play for a special cast, some re-arrangement might be found necessary. Most important of all, plays were liable to be revived, which means that the original author, or some other dramatist, would probably be employed to revise the manuscript; and revision, with its accompanying marginal additions and imperfect deletions, may leave strange traces in the printed text. Occasionally such revision would take the form of more or less drastic abridgment, as when a full-length play had to be cut down for a court performance.

Bearing all this in mind, an editor should generally be able to discover from the printed text a good deal about the nature of the 'copy' from which it was set up. He will be aided by literary considerations. For example, a chance reference to a character who does not elsewhere appear, a passage of 'verse' which refuses to scan, a violent and impossible dramatic *dénouement*, these and similar phenomena will excite his interest and arouse his curiosity. But a far more secure basis for his investigation is to be found in bibliographical analysis, which is scientific and independent of all questions of 'taste.' Roughly speaking a printed text is a faithful reproduction of the manuscript. The compositor's duty is to follow his 'copy'; and generally he does. When he finds 'Enter Will Kemp' therein, he prints it, without enquiring how this Kemp came to be walking about in Verona or Messina. If two versions of the same speech occur, because the author, in revising, has neglected to delete the older, both are likely to appear in print. Above all, the compositor has no means of distinguishing between verse and prose except by the line-arrangement in the manuscript. When therefore the verse-lining of a given passage is disturbed, it is fairly safe to assume that the 'copy' itself is to blame, and usually the best explanation is that the passage has been revised, cramped additions being written in the margin where lack of space forbade correct verse-lining. Eccentric line-arrangement, whether of verse or prose, is indeed a clue of great value to the bibliographer; and when it is found with a number of half-lines or broken lines of verse it is a certain sign of manuscript revision. For revision will generally involve, not merely marginal addition on some pages, but the complete re-writing of others; and the reviser is likely to betray his hand by leaving broken lines at the beginning or end of old speeches, when followed or preceded by additions. The necessary preliminary, therefore, to any definition of the printer's 'copy' is the collection of all bibliographical peculiarities which occur in the text. When this has been done, the editor will turn to the literary puzzles and consider how they fit in with his bibliographical findings.

But the 'copy' need not always be prompt-copy. After a play had been 'plotted' and the characters assigned, each player received his 'part,' with the cues, transcribed from the prompt-copy. If the prompt-copy were lost, or were for some other reason not available, it would be possible to reconstruct some kind of text for the printer by stringing together the 'parts.' At least one or two of the Folio texts suggest such an origin. At any rate it would be a grave error to regard the Folio as a unity in respect of the 'copy' employed. It is a *corpus Shakespearianum* made up of plays drawn from various sources, and each text therein must be judged on its merits, the merits being determined by the application of the principles of critical bibliography. As he proceeds, the textual editor of the present edition will attempt some provisional definition of the 'copy' for each of the original Shakespearian texts, in accordance with the foregoing principles. It will not always be possible, within the limits of his space, to give a complete account of the faith which is in him. But a brief statement of his general conclusions will be found at the end of every volume; the bibliographical and literary data upon which these conclusions rest will be brought out in the textual notes; and, at the conclusion of the edition, an exposition of the results of the survey will be attempted.

3. *Act and scene division: Line-numeration.*

None of the Quartos published during Shakespeare's life-time contains the conventional divisions which now appear in all modern texts. It would seem, therefore, that he did not work in acts and scenes; and the probability that most if not all these Quartos were printed from prompt-copies suggests that as long as he was at the Globe his plays were performed without breaks. On the other hand, only six undivided texts are to be found in the Folio, which was printed seven years after Shakespeare's death and a dozen years after his retirement to Stratford. The causes of this marked contrast between Folio and Quartos cannot be fully discussed here; but it is not difficult to discover at least a partial explanation. Act-divisions, which are of course classical in origin, are found in many sixteenth century dramatic texts, while some of the extant 'plots,' most of which belonged to the Admiral's men, prove that act-pauses were a recognised feature at certain theatres in Shakespeare's day. When therefore these divisions occur in Shakespeare's early plays, more especially when, as in *The Taming of the Shrew, King John* and I *Henry VI*, they crop up in a very irregular and haphazard fashion, they may be taken as evidence that he was revising other men's work and omitted to delete the act-headings. But, further, we have ten plays, previously published as Quartos, which the Folio has cut up into acts. Here the divisions are almost certainly due to the players, the stage-direction 'They sleepe all the Act' (i.e. the interval) which appears at the end of act III. of *A Midsummer-Night's Dream* being an important clue, and one eloquent of the shifts which a curtainless stage imposed upon those who attempted to divide the seamless texture of Shakespeare's dramas. And an explanation which fits these ten plays may be extended to other texts which exist in Folio version only. In short, it seems likely that such act-divisions are theatrical in origin, and arose from the practice of making four pauses during a performance, which were presumably introduced into Shakespeare's prompt-copies after he had left the Globe. Lastly, we have twelve Folio texts divided into scenes as well as acts. It is difficult to conceive any theatrical necessity for the insertion of scenes into a prompt-copy, but there was theatrical material which, if furnished with such prompt-copy, would render the introduction of scene-divisions into a printed text a very easy matter, though they might not, and in the Folio often do not, correspond with a modern editor's sense of literary or dramatic fitness. This theatrical material was the manuscript 'plot' of the play, which gave the entries and exits of the actors, and across which a line was drawn when the stage was left empty by one group of players to make room for another. With 'copy' in which the acts were marked, and with the 'plot' on which the 'exeunt omnes' lines were ruled, scene-division would present no difficulty to Jaggard.

That the divisions in the Folio are 'void of authority' and that Shakespeare wrote his plays 'in one unbroken continuity' was admitted by Dr Johnson in his preface of 1765, and Capell three years later pleaded for reformation. But they still persist in modern texts, though they are often dramatically absurd. In this edition they are wholly discarded, changes of place alone being marked by a space on the page. As however all modern glossaries, concordances, etc. employ line-numeration based on the traditional divisions, it has been found necessary, for purposes of reference, to adhere to it in the figures at the head of the page, which give the number of the first line. To the same end, the numerals in square brackets in the margin will indicate where the traditional acts and scenes begin. These numerals, it is hoped, will not only assist the reader in his references, but also serve, placed as they are alongside of a continuous text, to show how much or how little such breaks are in keeping with the intentions of Shakespeare.

4. *Punctuation and Stage-directions.*

The old texts were prompt-copy, more akin to operatic score than to modern literary drama. This explains the ungrammatical punctuation which, hitherto neglected or despised by editors, is now recognised as of the highest dramatic importance. The stops, brackets, capital letters in the Folio and Quartos are in fact stage-directions, in shorthand. They tell the actor when to pause and for how long, they guide his intonation, they indicate the emphatic word, often enough they denote 'stage-business.' The system was a simple one, though it became in Shakespeare's hands so delicate an instrument that it is very difficult to translate its finer touches into symbols which will commend themselves with ease to the modern eye. An attempt however has been made, and if the reader will glance through the note (pp. lvii–lx) in which details are explained, he will be able, when he comes to the text, to handle at least the more obvious ventages in Shakespeare's recorder and to catch something of the *tempo* of the verse as it sounded first of all in the poet's ear. If, on the other hand, he cares for none of these things, the punctuation we have adopted will not unduly disturb him.

The stops in the old texts, we have said, frequently stand for stage-business. As the original stage-directions are generally of the scantiest possible description, it is probable that 'business' was orally transmitted in Shakespeare's theatre. Indeed, a dramatic text with elaborate stage-directions lies under the suspicion of having been written by an author who was either not a player or unable to be present during the preparation for performance. With the aid of the dramatic punctuation it is now possible, in many places, to make at least a guess at the 'business' required. Where it has been felt that it would be of real help to the reader—and sometimes the text is unintelligible without it—such 'business' has been indicated by stage-directions. The bulk of the stage-directions which appear in modern editions are the creation of editors and critics, and we are therefore only carrying the process a step further—to what we believe to be its logical conclusion. While we are fully aware of the risks we run in such an undertaking, the attempt has so greatly deepened our own appreciation of Shakespeare's purposes that we are encouraged to hope that the results may not be found altogether impertinent.

A strong and healthy reaction has recently set in against superfluity of scenery at performances of Shakespeare's plays, and it is possible that objection may be taken to another of our innovations, viz. the *mise-en-scène* stage-direction. It should be remembered, however, that this edition is intended not for the Elizabethan actor but for the modern reader, and that a play-book is a very different thing from a moving audible pageant. In our opinion the almost complete absence of stage-directions in the printed text is one of the chief obstacles to the appreciation of Shakespeare by his own countrymen. It would appear from the doctrines of some extremists that they believe Shakespeare never thought of any background except the theatre-boards at the Globe. But as a matter of fact he almost always formed a clear-cut and definite picture of the surroundings amid which his characters moved, and it is generally possible to reconstruct this scenery from incidental references in the play. In attempting this, we shall again only be completing the process already begun by previous editors.

Stage-directions taken from the original texts will be placed in inverted commas, so as to distinguish them from our additions.

5. *Spellings and Abbreviations.*

In this edition the spelling of the old texts has been modernised, save for a few Shakespearian forms which seemed worth preserving either for the sake of their quaintness or because the original gives help to the meaning, ease to the scansion or grace to a rhyme. Little is lost by modernisation, for the simple reason that the spelling of the Folio and Quartos is normally not that of Shakespeare. The faithful compositor followed his 'copy' it is true; but he was bound to alter his authors' spelling if he was to get through his day's work at all, seeing that every author in that age spelt as he liked and it would have been infinitely laborious to set up each word exactly as it appeared in the 'copy.' Yet if a word in the manuscript happens to catch the compositor's eye, the author's spelling is likely to get into print through inadvertence. Thus by observing spellings which are unusual for reputable compositors of Shakespeare's day, it is possible to learn a good deal of an author's orthographic habits. A collection of such abnormal spellings as are to be found in the seventeen Good Quartos has been made by the textual editor, and has proved of considerable value in the preparation of this text.

Shakespeare had his own spelling; he also abbreviated freely, the old texts being full of contracted forms, which modern editors have generally treated in a half-hearted and inconsistent fashion, though they are clearly of great importance as regards verse-scansion. Thanks to a recent attempt by the advocate of a new prosody to get rid of them altogether, we have been led to examine them closely in the light of contemporary usage and to weigh carefully the bibliographical and philological evidence in their favour. Our conclusion is that they are undoubtedly Shakespearian in origin, and that it is therefore an editor's duty to retain them all, except where they are obvious misprints. Since however final *-ed* has long ceased to be syllabic in modern English pronunciation, except after *d* and *t*, it seemed superfluous to contract here. We have therefore always printed it in full, accenting it where poetic or obsolete syllabification is required.

6. *Misprints, Shakespeare's handwriting, Emendation.*

It is a cardinal principle of critical bibliography that when anything is wrong with the text, the blame should be laid rather on the 'copy' than on the compositor. This principle applies to most forms of misprint. But there are certain types of misprint for which compositors may be held responsible. Such are: (1) The omission

of single lines. (2) The omission of words. (3) The alteration of a word by assimilation to a neighbouring word
of like sound or spelling. (4) Small verbal alterations
due to an attempt to carry too many words in the head.
Closely connected with this class is the large quantity of
grammatical errors occurring ·in the texts, which no
editor of Shakespeare has yet faced squarely. That Shakespeare's grammar was always in accordance with modern
usage no one will be bold enough to maintain. But it
can hardly be doubted that many solecisms were introduced by his printers which he would not have counte-
nanced.

We pass to misprints for which Shakespeare must be
held at least partly responsible; and their name is legion.
No less instructive to an editor than the abnormal
spellings are the obvious misprints which occur by the
hundred in the Good Quartos, misprints which have been
corrected in all modern editions. A list of these has been
made and classified by the textual editor, and such a list
shows us the kind of slips to which Shakespeare's pen was
most prone. The principal types are as follows: (1) A large
class of misprints due to confusion set up by the mal-
formation of minim-letters, especially when they occur
in combination. In the 'English' hand, which Shakespeare wrote, minim-letters are *m, n, u, i, c, w, r*, and it is
clear that he frequently neglected to count his strokes
when writing these. (2) A closely related class due to a
confusion of *a* with *n, u*, and other minim-letters. This is
to be explained by Shakespeare's habit of neglecting to
close the top of the *a*, thus leaving it a virtual *u* or *n*.
(3) What may be called *e:d* misprints. These are very
common, and are important as proving that Shakespeare
wrote the 'English' and not the 'Italian' hand which
we now employ, since the only difference between
e and *d* in the 'English' style was one of size, a difference which Shakespeare was not careful to observe.
It is probable that something like half the corruptions in

the Shakespearian texts may be attributed to this cause.
(4) *e : o* misprints. The chief difference between these two
letters, in 'English' script, is that the *e* is linked with the
letter following and the *o* is not; they are therefore very
liable to be confused when a writer is working quickly.
(5) *o : a* misprints. Most of these occur in cases where a
minim-letter follows the *a* or *o*, and are probably due to
a trick of the pen by which the upright of the *a* became
detached from the body of the letter, so as to give something which might be taken for *oi* or *or*.

To these main classes should be added mistakes due to
confusion between long-headed letters of various kinds
(e.g. *f*, long *s*, *l*, *t*), and between tailed letters such as *g*, *y*,
h, errors likely to occur in printing from any 'English'
hand, as indeed are some of those mentioned above.

All this has an important bearing upon the question of textual corruption; and our lists of spellings
and misprints give us a scientific instrument for dealing
with it. The spellings are quite as useful as the misprints since unless we have some idea of the letters
which Shakespeare actually wrote on paper, it is often
impossible to see how the compositor went wrong. When
a passage in the text lies under strong suspicion of corruption, the suspect word or phrase should first of all be
written out in Shakespearian script and Shakespearian
spelling. This done, the right reading will quite often
leap to the eye, since the trouble is generally caused by a
simple minim or *e : d* misprint, or perhaps may be just a
question of misdivision of a word. If the corruption
proves a stubborn one, other classes of misprint must be
brought to bear upon the problem, and various com-
binations of letters tried. Finally the results of this application of the principle of the *ductus litterarum* must
be put to the literary test, by reference to the context,
and by the aid of the *New English Dictionary* which will
supply, or withhold, contemporary support for the suggested reading. But the literary criterion, though of

course essential, should not be brought in until the last stage, when bibliography and palaeography have done their work. The basis of the whole business, in short, is the handwriting of Shakespeare; and that it is now possible not only to imagine but actually to write this hand is due to the researches of Sir Edward Maunde Thompson.

By the aid of these new tools, time-honoured textual cruxes have been attacked and fresh ones brought to light in the present edition, so that a number of emendations will be suggested in the notes to each play. As, however, the method is here employed for the first time, and has therefore yet to receive the general approval of scholars, no emendations have been admitted into the text itself, unless (*a*) the original reading makes nonsense of a crucial dramatic passage, so that there is virtually a hole which requires filling up; (*b*) the editors feel assured that no alternative to the reading they propose is possible; or (*c*) the reading which appears exceedingly likely on palaeographical or bibliographical grounds has already been suggested by some previous critic of repute. Corrupt passages of importance, whether emended or otherwise, will be marked with an obelisk in the text, the original spelling being given in some cases to enable the reader to follow out the problem for himself. Every departure from the original text will be recorded in the notes at the end of the volume. And the facsimile of a passage from the 'Shakespearian' scene in the *Sir Thomas More* manuscript is given in this volume to illustrate the kind of writing in which the plays were first penned.

7. *Verse-arrangement.*

Owing chiefly to the practice of marginal revision the old texts frequently give us passages of verse incorrectly divided or printed in prose. Many of these passages have been rectified by previous editors, but we have found that a certain amount still remains to be done. On the other hand, the reviser is not always Shakespeare, and lines of prose (generally designed to cover a 'cut') are liable to be found embedded in the verse. Not infrequently editors have tinkered at these in the vain effort to fit them into the metrical context. We have left them alone, as prose, or with the line-arrangement which the original gives them; for, lament them as we may, they are of interest as bibliographical evidence.

8. *Notes and Glossary*.

The notes at the end of each volume will be mainly textual, though occasionally they will deal with the elucidation of quibbles (to which special attention has been given) and of other passages which cannot conveniently be grouped alphabetically in the glossary. In preparing both notes and glossary the editors have attempted to take full advantage of the opportunities now open to Shakespearian scholars in those two noble compilations, issued by the University of Oxford, *Shakespeare's England* and *The New English Dictionary*.

D. W.

THE TEMPEST

The Tempest is the first play in the First Folio of 1623; and this, for aught anybody knows—indeed almost certainly—was its first appearance in print. The Folio, at any rate, supplies our only text. Chronologically it is almost the last, if not the very last, that Shakespeare wrote. The Folio editors, Heminge and Condell, old friends of his and fellow-actors, may have given it pride of place for this pious reason, or possibly because it had won a striking success at Court when presented there in the winter of 1612–13, among many entertainments that graced the betrothal and nuptials of the Princess Elizabeth with the Prince Palatine Elector. John Heminge, as foreman of Shakespeare's old Company, was paid by Lord Harrington, Treasurer of the Chamber of King James I, 'upon the councells warrant, dated at Whitehall xx⁰ die Mai, 1613' his bill for producing 'foureteene severall playes' in the course of these festivities which were numerous and so costly as to embarrass His Majesty's exchequer. The entry (*Vertue MSS*) specifies these plays, and *The Tempest* comes sixth on the list[1].

[1] In 1842 Peter Cunningham, a clerk in the Audit Office, discovered (or professed to discover) in the cellars of Somerset House two Account Books of the Revels Office, for 1604–5 and 1611–12, and in the latter an entry that *The Tempest* was presented at Whitehall before the King on Hallowmas night 1611. The document, subsequently impounded by the British Museum and long suspected for a forgery, has been well vindicated by Mr Ernest Law (*Some Supposed Shakespeare Forgeries*, 1911), though we understand that a few scholars yet doubt its authenticity. Authentic or not, the entry leaves us free to believe that, *as we have it*, *The Tempest* was designed for the winter festivities of 1612–13. That there is good reason to suppose its existence in previous form (or forms) we attempt to show on pp. 79–85 of this volume.

It is pleasant and certainly not impossible to believe that, as Heminge and Condell have preserved it for us, this play was written-up expressly for the betrothal —and presented on Dec. 27, 1612, the betrothal night— of the incomparable Queen of Hearts whose name in story is Elizabeth of Bohemia,

> design'd
> Th'eclipse and glory of her kind.

For 'beauty vanishes, beauty passes,' but the charm of this woman still fascinates the imagination almost as in her life-time it won and compelled the souls of men to champion her sorrowful fortunes. That it did this—that it laid on the nobler spirits of her time a spell potent to extravagance and yet so finely apportioned as almost to serve us now for a test and gauge of their nobility—no reader of early seventeenth century biography will deny. The evidence is no less frequent than startling. It would almost seem that no 'gentleman' could come within the aura but he knelt to Elizabeth of Bohemia, her sworn knight: that either he followed thenceforth to the last extremity, proud only to serve, or, called away, he departed as one who had looked upon a vision which changed all the values of life, who had beheld a kingdom of the soul in which self and this world were well lost for a dream. We may see this strange conversion in Wotton; we may trace it in the careers of Donne, of Dudley Carleton and (with a postscript of morose disillusion) Lord Herbert of Cherbury. We may read it, youthfully and romantically expressed in this well-authenticated story:

A company of young men of the Middle Temple met together for supper; and when the wine went round the first man rose, and holding a cup in one hand and a sword in the other, pledged the health of the distressed Princess, the Lady Elizabeth; and having drunk, he kissed the sword, and laying hand upon it, took a solemn oath to live and die in her service. His ardour kindled the whole company. They all rose, and from one to another the cup and sword went round till each had taken the pledge.

We may see this exuberance carried into steady practice by Lord Craven, a Lord Mayor's son, who having poured blood and money in her service, laid his last wealth at her feet to provide her a stately refuge and a home. Through all the story she—grand-daughter of Mary of Scotland, mother of Rupert of the Rhine—rides reckless, feckless, spendthrift, somehow ineffably great; conquering all hearts near her, that

> —Enamour'd do wish so they might
> But enjoy such a sight,
> That they still were to run by her side
> Thoro' swords, thoro' seas, whither she would ride,

lifting all those gallant hearts to ride with her, for a desperate cause, despising low ends, ignoble gain; to ride with her down and nobly over the last lost edge of the world.

We may take it almost for a certainty that—in whatever previous form or forms presented—this play *as we have it* was the play enacted at Court to grace the Princess Elizabeth's betrothal. No argument from internal evidence conflicts with this. Gonzalo's description of his ideal Commonwealth (2. 1. 146 *sqq.*) comes out of Florio's translation of Montaigne, first published in 1603[1]: and the name 'Caliban' suggests the essay 'Of the Cannibales' from which Gonzalo derived his wisdom. Ben Jonson most likely has a side thrust at *The Tempest* (and at *The Winter's Tale*) in his Introduction to *Bartholomew Fair* (acted in October, 1614): 'If there be never a Servant-monster i' the *Fayre*, who can help it, he sayes; nor a nest of *Antiques*? Hee is loth to make nature afraid in

---

[1] The British Museum once supposed itself to contain Shakespeare's own copy of this book, but found the autograph to be a forgery.

his *Playes*, like those that beget *Tales*, *Tempests*, and such like *Drolleries*.' Further, we can easily allow the play to contain many passages suggested by the mis-adventure of the Virginian voyage of 1609, when a fleet of nine ships and five hundred colonists under com-mand of Sir Thomas Gates and Sir George Somers was dispersed by a gale and the flagship, the *Sea-Adventure*, went ashore on the coast of Bermudas, her crew wonder-fully escaping. That Shakespeare used at least one or two out of several pamphlets dealing with this wreck (by Silvester Jourdain, by William Strachey, and by 'advise and direction of the Councell of Virginia'—to mention no others) stands above question. But nothing of this is inconsistent either with the play's having been presented by the King's Players on Hallowmas, 1611, or with its having been recast and 'revived' for the festivities of the Princess Elizabeth's betrothal.

Nothing forbids our imagination to repeople the Banqueting House and recall this bride, this paragon, to seat her in the front rank of the ghostly audience: to watch her, a moment before the curtain opens, a little reclined, her jewelled wrists, like Cassiopeia's, laid along the arms of her chair; or still to watch her as the play proceeds and she—affianced and, by admission, in love with her bridegroom—leans forward with parted lips to follow the loves of Ferdinand and Miranda.

Those who must always be searching for a 'source' of every plot of Shakespeare's (as though he could invent nothing!) will be disappointed in *The Tempest*. Thomas Warton (or rather, Warton misunderstood by Malone) started one false hare by a note in his *History of English Poetry*, vol. III. (1781), that he had been 'informed by the late Mr Collins of Chichester'— that is, Collins the poet—that Shakespeare's *Tempest* was formed on a 'favourite romance,' *Aurelio and Isabella*, printed in 1586 (one volume) in Italian, French and English, and again in 1588 in Italian, Spanish, French and English; the Spanish of Flores being the original. But Collins' mind was darkening towards madness at the time: and *Aurelio*, when found, contained nothing in common with *The Tempest*. Others have followed the clue of a German play, *Die Schöne Sidea*, written by one Jacob Ayrer, a notary of Nuremberg, who died in 1605. There is a magician in this drama who is also a prince—Prince Ludolph: he has a demon or familiar spirit: he has an only daughter too. The son of Ludolph's enemy becomes his prisoner, his sword being held in sheath by the magician's art. Later, the young man is forced to bear logs for Ludolph's daughter. She falls in love with him, and all ends happily. The resemblances to *The Tempest* are obvious: and that there was some actual thread of connexion appears the likelier when we note that 'mountain' and 'silver,' two names of the spirit hounds which Prospero and Ariel set upon the 'foul conspiracy' (4. 1. 256), occur in an invocation of Prince Ludolph's in the German play. It may be that Shakespeare used Ayrer's play; for the English Comedians were at Nuremberg in 1604, where they may have seen *Die Schöne Sidea*, to bring home the story. But it is just as likely that Ayrer's is a version of one they took from England to Germany. And, after all, what fairy-tale or folk-tale is commoner, the world over, than that which combines a witch, or wizard, an only daughter, an adventurous prince caught and bound to carry logs, etc., with pity and confederate love to counteract the spell and bring all right in the end?

When we turn to Shakespeare's handling of this story, we first admire that which all must admire, the enchantment wherein he clothes it, the poetic feeling wherewith he suffuses it. Magic and music meet in *The Tempest* and are so wedded that none can put them asunder.

That was the chirp of Ariel
You heard, as overhead it flew;
The farther going, more to dwell
And wing our green to wed our blue;
But whether note of joy, or knell,
Not his own Father-singer knew;
Nor yet can any mortal tell,
Save only that it shivers through;
The breast of us a sounded shell,
The blood of us a lighted dew.

But when we have paid homage to all this, on second thoughts we may find the firm anatomy beneath the robe—the mere craftmanship—scarcely less wonderful. For *The Tempest* accepts and masters an extreme technical difficulty. No one can react Shakespeare's later plays in a block without recognising that the subject which constantly engaged his mind towards the close of life was *Reconciliation*, with pardon and atonement for the sins or mistakes of one generation in the young love of the children and in their promise. This is the true theme of *Pericles, Cymbeline, The Winter's Tale, The Tempest*, successively. But the process of reconciliation— especially when effected through the appeal of sons and daughters—is naturally a slow one, and therefore extremely difficult to translate into drama, which handles 'the two hours' traffic of our stage' and therefore must almost necessarily rely on the piling of circumstance and character upon one crisis and its swiftest possible resolution. In attempting to condense such 'romantic' stories of reconciliation as he had in his mind, Shakespeare was in fact taking up the glove thrown down by Sir Philip Sidney in his pretty mockery of bad playwrights.

Now of time they are much more liberall. For ordinary it is that two young Princes fall in love. After many traverses she is got with child, delivered of a faire boy, he is lost, groweth a man, falls in love, and is ready to get another child, and all this in two hours' space; which how absurd it is in sence, even sence may imagine, and Arte hath taught, and all ancient examples justified.

The time supposed to be occupied by the action of *Pericles* is about sixteen years. *The Winter's Tale* has an interval of about sixteen years between its third and fourth Acts. The chronology of *Cymbeline* is baffling and in places absurd; yet it must cover many months. The once famous Unity of Time is certainly no 'law': but it *is* a grace of drama. And after falling back on such make-shifts as ancient Gower in *Pericles* and Father Time himself in *The Winter's Tale*, of a sudden in *The Tempest* our artist triumphantly 'does the trick.' The whole action of the play, with the whole tale of ancient wrong unfolded, the whole company of injuring and injured gathered into a knot, the whole machinery of revenge converted to forgiveness—all this is managed in about three hours of imagined time, or scarcely more than the time of its actual representation on the stage.

The *clou* of this feat of stage-craft lies in the famous *protasis* of the second scene, where Prospero so naturally unfolds all the preliminaries to his daughter. For exquisite use of *protasis* this may be compared with the second scene of *Hamlet*. Many critics have praised it: but we hope that by a few simple stage-directions we have managed to suggest a beauty which the most of them have missed—the abstracted mind of Miranda as she listens with a kind of *feyness* to the story so important on which her father, having chosen and prepared the moment, so impatiently insists. It is, to our thinking, most necessary to realise that Miranda is all the while less absorbed by this important story than by the sea, out of which her fairy prince is surely coming, though his coming be scarcely surmised as yet. We shall not understand this play, lacking to understand how young impulse forestalls and takes charge, outrunning our magician's deliberate contrivance. When Ferdinand and Miranda actually meet

> At the first sight
> They have changed eyes.

For another point, not over-subtle, which the critics would seem to·have overlooked: It is clear to us that the enchantment of the island purposely makes its appearance correspond with the several natures of the ship-wrecked men who come ashore. Gonzalo, the 'honest old councillor,' finds 'our garments rather new dyed than stained with salt water.' But Antonio and Sebastian cannot see them so. To him 'how lush and lusty the grass looks! how green!' Antonio, the total jaundiced villain, sees it 'tawny,' the half-corrupt Sebastian detects 'an eye of green in't'—and so on throughout. Gonzalo indeed is one of Shakespeare's minor triumphs. He is not left—as Antigonus, his counterpart in *The Winter's Tale* was left—to perish after his kind deed. It was done long ago: but he survives, still in his character of loyal-hearted servant, still active in loyalty, which in its turn advances the action of the play. Is it not a delicate stroke that, when Miranda first hears the story of her casting away, of all the shipwrecked company near at hand, though she knows it not, this old councillor is the man she (being heart-whole yet) most desires to see? So in the end he is not only one of the company that awakes Miranda's cry of

> O wonder!
> How many goodly creatures are there here!
> How beauteous mankind is! O brave new world,
> That has such people in't!

But for him is reserved the final blessing,

> Look down, you gods,
> And on this couple drop a blesséd crown!

so unmistakably echoing Hermione's invocation in *The Winter's Tale*,

> You gods, look down,
> And from your sacred vials pour your graces
> Upon my daughter's head!

Caliban has been over-philosophised by the critics (with Renan and Browning to support them). The truth would seem to be that Shakespeare, like a true demiurge, had a tendency to love his creations, and none the less those whom he shows us as gross, carnal, earthy. If it be not unfair to drag Falstaff into the comparison, then even as none of us can help loving Falstaff, so few of us shall we say?—if Caliban came fawning about our legs, would be disinclined to pay him on the head with a 'Good dog! Good monster!' Our sense of justice, too, helps this instinct: for, after all, Caliban has the right of it when he snarls,

> I must eat my dinner.
> This island's mine, by Sycorax my mother,
> Which thou tak'st from me:

—and we must remind ourselves that in 1611 and thereabouts this dispossession of the aborigine was a very present event, however feebly it might touch the imagination, to trouble the conscience, of our valorous circumnavigators and colonists. Shakespeare, as we conceive him, differed from Rousseau in most ways, and not least in immunity from any temptation to construct an ideal portrait of the 'noble savage.' But no man can be catholic as Shakespeare was without being fair, and so (as Hazlitt noted) while the nature of Caliban is the essence of grossness, there is not a particle of vulgarity in it. Few have remarked how admirably significant as a set-off to Caliban is Stephano, type of his predestined conquerors, the tarry, racy, absolute British seaman, staggering through this isle of magic with a bottle, staring, hiccoughing back against Ariel's invisible harp—

> The master, the swabber, the bos'n and I...

in extremity to be counted on for the fine confused last

word of our mercantile marine, 'Every man shift for all the rest.' It is hard to over-estimate the solidarity of Stephano and the 'value' it gives to the whole fairy picture[1].

Many critics have lost their hearts to Miranda and no one has excelled Coleridge's praise in delicacy of insight. Let us add but this—Shakespeare has contrived to mould her of frank goodness and yet present her as fascinating, captivating by touches so noble that one can hardly conceive the part adequately rendered save by a princess in real life as noble as she—an Elizabeth of Bohemia, for example. She moves to her appointed happiness with fairies and music about her; but she sees no fairies, sings no song, simply walks straight as the dictate of her heart directs, and, so walking, steps straight beyond the magic her father has woven. This incomparable play contains nothing more subtly simple than her unconscious, quite fearless, outstripping of all Prospero's premeditated art. He has drawn around the island a magic circle as that which Ferdinand cannot step across. The play, like *A Midsummer-Night's Dream*, plainly celebrates a betrothal and marches to the fruition of marriage joy. There is much music in both: in both the fairies are made abetters. But whereas in *A Midsummer-Night's Dream* the fairies were Warwickshire elves, playing their pranks anarchically, at their own sweet fancy, to befool mortals, the more rarefied spirits of *The Tempest* obey, under threat, a mortal's compulsion. But Miranda is for the world, gently but fearlessly; on the primal instinct that makes homes, builds and

---

[1] In the list of *dramatis personae* Stephano is merely 'a drunken Butler,' and plainly he does not belong to the working crew of the ship, all of whom Ariel has stowed under hatches. But that he was a seaman his opening song and the general saltiness of his language make pretty plain. He would seem to have been withdrawn and given a livery (as the custom was) as superintendent of the King's temporary cellar on shipboard.

populates cities, recreates and rules the race. Some
have objected that this play does not develop; that
within Prospero's charmed circle, for the space of three
hours, all stands still. In truth a great deal happens,
and the ease of its happening is a trick of most cunning
preparation.

Who is Prospero? Is he perchance Destiny itself; the
master-spirit that has brooded invisible and moved on
the deep waters of the greater tragedies, and now comes
to shore on a lost nest of the main to sun himself; laying
by his robe of darkness to play, at his great ease, one last
trick before following the way of the old gods? Is he (as
Campbell the poet was the first to suggest) Shakespeare
himself, in this last of his plays breaking his wand and
drowning his book 'deeper than did ever plummet
sound'? The lights in the banqueting house are out:
the Princess Elizabeth is dust: and as for the island con-
jured out of the sea for a night's entertainment—

> From that day forth the Isle has been
> By wandering sailors never seen.

Ariel has nestled to the bat's back and slid away following
summer or else 'following darkness like a dream.' But
still this play abides, after three hundred years, eloquent
of Shakespeare's slow sunsetting through dream after
dream of reconciliation; forcing tears, not by 'pity and
terror' but by sheer beauty; with a royal sense of the
world, how it passes away, with a catch at the heart sur-
mising hope in what is to come. And still the sense is
royal: we feel that we are greater than we know. So in
the surge of our emotion, as on the surges rounding
Prospero's island, is blown a spray, a mist. Actually it
dims our eyes: and as we brush it away, there rides on it a
rainbow; and its colours are chastened wisdom, wistful
charity; with forgiveness, tender ruth for all men and
women growing older, and perennial trust in young love.

Q.

A NOTE ON PUNCTUATION

In the main, the punctuation of the old texts is Shakespeare's, or at worst that of the play-house. No doubt the compositor had his share too; in plays hurriedly written perhaps a large one, in others such as *Hamlet* or *The Tempest* a small one—probably little more than the addition of certain commas. In either event the framework is Shakespearian. This punctuation is dramatic, that is to say it is a question of pause, emphasis and intonation; and is quite independent of syntax. A comma indicates a short pause, a semicolon a longer one, a colon one longer still, and a full-stop—a *full* stop, which sometimes occurs in the middle of a sentence. Further, absence of punctuation, where a modern reader would expect to find it, implies rapid delivery. Brackets, on the other hand, affect intonation rather than speed. Often they denote the drop in the voice which a parenthesis demands; but there are many beautiful instances which mark a much more significant change of tone: a hushed whisper, a touch of anxiety, a note of tenderness, surprise or awe. In the same way the pause, especially with the semicolon, the colon or the period, often needs filling by a sob, a kiss, or by other and lengthier 'business.' As he wrote Shakespeare had the living voice ever sounding in his ears, the flesh and blood of his creations ever moving before his eyes.

To translate this exquisite pointing into symbols convenient to the modern eye is no easy task. We have retained as much of the original system as possible; but, inasmuch as it was non-syntactical in character, to keep it all would have tended to bewilderment and confusion. Thus we have been forced, reluctantly, to compromise, as follows:

Full-stop. When this occurs at the end of a speech no change has been made. When it is internal, it invariably denotes a long pause, often for stage-business, and we have shown its presence by four dots, thus ....

It follows that internal full-stops which occur in this text are not Shakespearian, but introduced for grammatical reasons, being generally a substitute for an original comma.

Colon. Except for obvious misprints, this has been retained, either in its original form or as three dots, thus ... The translation by dots has been found useful at the end of a speech, in places where a colon is grammatically impossible, or where for dramatic reasons it seemed well to bring the pause prominently before the reader's attention.

Semicolon. This is often difficult to distinguish from the colon on the one hand and the comma on the other. It has been retained wherever possible; at times, however, it has been translated by a dash, and at others by three dots, as with the colon. In a prose play, like *The Merry Wives*, it has occasionally been found necessary to substitute a semicolon for a comma.

Comma. Where this appears to possess special dramatic significance, it is given as a dash, or as a couple of dashes on either side of a word or phrase. Obviously, however, we have been obliged to take greater liberties with this stop than with the others. A large number of fresh commas have been introduced into the text for grammatical reasons; original ones have been omitted for a like cause; sometimes full-stops or, less often, semicolons, have been substituted.

Exclamation-marks. Shakespeare was very sparing in his use of these; and, though in scenes full of movement we have felt compelled to introduce some which do not appear in the old texts, we have dispensed with hundreds of unauthorised examples of this rhetorical flourish which have hitherto found a place in modern editions. It should here be noted that in the old texts a question-mark often did service for a note of exclamation, and that the printers only had small stocks of the latter, which partly explains its infrequency.

Brackets. Really significant instances of this have been retained; commas have been substituted where simple parenthesis alone is implied; between these two extremes lie a number of examples in which a couple of dashes and often an exclamation-mark have taken the place of the brackets.

The single bracket occasionally found at the beginning of speeches in the text is a device of our own to mark off subsidiary dialogue or a series of 'asides' from the main dialogue.

Emphasis-capitals. Shakespeare generally conveyed emphasis by the use of the pause. Sometimes, however, he indicated the emphatic word by beginning it with a capital letter. The Folio teems with emphasis-capitals, which are probably due in the main to an affection for capitals among seventeenth century compositors; anyhow it is certain that, in bulk, they are non-Shakespearian. Yet here and there we can catch a Shakespearian emphasis even in the Folio, while in the Quartos, where they are far less frequent, the dramatist's hand is more often in evidence. Where we have felt tolerably certain that Shakespeare himself intended emphasis we have printed the word with spaced lettering.

Inverted commas. These are sometimes used in the old texts, at the beginning of the line, to draw attention to maxims or proverbial 'sentences,' and will be retained in the double form the original gives. Single inverted commas are our own and will be introduced to indicate quotation. Stage-directions in inverted commas are those taken direct from the Folio or Quartos.

The Tempest is a particularly beautiful example of dramatic pointing; and we feel confident that if, after glancing at this brief note, the reader will turn to the second scene and follow for a moment or two the pause-effects in the exquisite dialogue between Miranda and her father, he will not only master its principles without difficulty but will become a complete convert to Shakespearian punctuation.

D. W.

THE TEMPEST

'The scene, an uninhabited island'

CHARACTERS IN THE PLAY

ALONSO, *King of Naples*

SEBASTIAN, *his brother*

PROSPERO, *the right Duke of Milan*

ANTONIO, *his brother, the usurping Duke of Milan*

FERDINAND, *son to the King of Naples*

GONZALO, *an honest old Councillor*

ADRIAN *and* FRANCISCO, *Lords*

CALIBAN, *a savage and deformed slave*

TRINCULO, *a Jester*

STEPHANO, *a drunken Butler*

SHIP-MASTER

BOATSWAIN

Mariners

MIRANDA, *daughter to Prospero*

ARIEL, *an airy Spirit*

IRIS
CERES
JUNO } *Spirits*
Nymphs
Reapers

Homework

The character of Prospero is at one and
the same time the simplest and most
complexed that Shakespeare ever
created. Discuss

THE TEMPEST

[1.1.] '*A tempestuous noise of thunder and lightning heard.*'
The waist of a ship is seen, seas breaking over it.

A SHIP-MASTER: A BOATSWAIN.

Master [*from the poop-deck*]. Bos'n!
Boatswain [*in the waist*]. Here, master: what cheer?
Master. Good: speak to th' mariners: fall to't—yarely—
or we run ourselves aground. Bestir, bestir.

[*he returns to the helm*

Master's whistle heard. Mariners come aft.

Boatswain. Heigh my hearts! cheerly, cheerly my hearts
...yare, yare...take in the topsail...tend to th' master's
whistle... [*to the gale*] Blow till thou burst thy wind—if
room enough!

'*ALONSO, SEBASTIAN, ANTONIO, FERDINAND,*
GONZALO, and others' *come on deck.*

Alonso. Good bos'n, have care, Where's the master?
Play the men.   10
Boatswain. I pray now, keep below.
Antonio. Where is the master, bos'n?
Boatswain. Do you not hear him? You mar our labour.
Keep your cabins: you do assist the storm.
Gonzalo. Nay, good, be patient.
Boatswain.   When the sea is...Hence!
What care these roarers for the name of king?
To cabin...silence...trouble us not!
Gonzalo. Good, yet remember whom thou hast aboard.
Boatswain. None that I more love than myself...You are
a Councillor—if you can command these elements to   20

silence, and work the peace of the present, we will not
hand a rope more. Use your authority...If you cannot,
give thanks you have lived so long, and make yourself
ready in your cabin for the mischance of the hour, if it
so hap....

Cheerly, good hearts...Out of our way, I say.

[*he runs forward*

Gonzalo [*his speech interrupted as the ship pitches*]. I have
great comfort from this fellow...Methinks he hath no
drowning mark upon him, his complexion is perfect gal-
30 lows...Stand fast, good Fate, to his hanging, make the
rope of his destiny our cable, for our own doth little
advantage...If he be not born to be hanged, our case is
miserable.

BOATSWAIN *comes aft: courtiers retreat before him*
to their cabins.

Boatswain. Down with the topmast...yare, lower,
lower! bring her to try with main-course.... ['*A cry*' *is
heard below*]. A plague upon this howling...they are
louder than the weather, or our office...

SEBASTIAN, ANTONIO, *and* GONZALO *return.*

Yet again? What do you here? Shall we give o'er and
drown? Have you a mind to sink?

40 *Sebastian.* A pox o' your throat, you bawling, blasphe-
mous, incharitable dog!

Boatswain. Work you, then.   [*he turns from them*

Antonio. Hang, cur; hang, you whoreson, insolent
noise-maker! we are less afraid to be drowned than
thou art.

Gonzalo. I'll warrant him for drowning, though the ship
were no stronger than a nutshell, and as leaky as an unstaunched wench.

Boatswain [*shouting*]. Lay her a-hold, a-hold! Set her
two courses. Off to sea again! lay her off!   50

*The ship strikes. Fireballs flame along the rigging and
      from beak to stern. 'Enter mariners wet.'*

Mariners. All lost! to prayers, to prayers! all lost!
Boatswain [*slowly pulling out a bottle*]. What, must
our mouths be cold?
Gonzalo. The king and prince at prayers. Let's
      assist them,
For our case is as theirs.
Sebastian.   I am out of patience.
Antonio. We are merely cheated of our lives by
      drunkards—
This wide-chopped rascal—would thou mightst lie
      drowning
The washing of ten tides!
Gonzalo.   He'll be hanged yet,
Though every drop of water swear against it,
And gape at wid'st to glut him.
'*A confused noise*' *below*   Mercy on us!—   60
We split, we split!—Farewell, my wife and children!—
Farewell, brother!—We split, we split, we split!
Antonio. Let's all sink wi' th' king.
Sebastian.   Let's take leave of him. [*they go below*
Gonzalo. Now would I give a thousand furlongs of sea—
for an acre of barren ground…long heath, brown furze,
any thing…The wills above be done, but I would fain
die a dry death!

*A crowd bursts upon deck, making for the ship's side, in the
glare of the fireballs. Of a sudden these are quenched. A loud
cry of many voices.*

Greek Idea of the unities
Narrated— Events which happened before
the Storm .

6   THE TEMPEST   I.2.I

[I.2.] *The Island. A green plat of undercliff, approached by*
a path descending through a grove of lime-trees alongside the
upper cliff, in the face of which is the entrance of a tall cave,
curtained. MIRANDA, *gazing out to sea:* PROSPERO, *in*
wizard's mantle and carrying a staff, comes from the cave.

Miranda [turning]. If by your art—my dearest father—
    you have
Put the wild waters in this roar—allay them:
The sky, it seems, would pour down stinking pitch,
But that the sea, mounting to th' welkin's cheek,
Dashes the fire out....O! I have suffered
With those that I saw suffer: A brave vessel,

                                    [*in a whisper*
(Who had no doubt some noble creature in her!)   *hint of whats*
Dashed all to pieces: [*sobbing*] O the cry did knock   *to come*
Against my very heart...poor souls, they perished....
10 Had I been any god of power, I would
Have sunk the sea within the earth, or e'er
It should the good ship so have swallowed, and
The fraughting souls within her.
    Prospero.   Be collected,
No more amazement: Tell your piteous heart
There's no harm done.
    Miranda.   O woe the day!
    Prospero.   No harm:
I have done nothing, but in care of thee
(Of thee, my dear one; thee, my daughter) who
Art ignorant of what thou art....nought knowing
Of whence I am...nor that I am more better
20 Than Prospero, master of a full poor cell,
And thy no greater father.
    Miranda [her eyes on the sea again]. More to know
Did never meddle with my thoughts.

Prospero.   'Tis time
I should inform thee farther: Lend thy hand
And pluck my magic garment from me...So,
                              [*he lays aside his mantle*
Lie there my art: Wipe thou thine eyes, have comfort,
The direful spectacle of the wreck, which touched
The very virtue of compassion in thee...
I have with such provision in mine art
†So safely ordered, that there is no soil,
No, not so much perdition as an hair,   30
Betid to any creature in the vessel
Which thou heard'st cry, which thou saw'st sink:
     Sit down,
For thou must now know farther.
    Miranda.   You have often
Begun to tell me what I am, but stopped,
And left me to a bootless inquisition,
Concluding, 'Stay: not yet.'
    Prospero.   The hour's now come,
The very minute bids thee ope thine ear,
Obey, and be attentive....
           [*he sits on a bench of rock, Miranda beside him*
                    Canst thou remember
A time before we came unto this cell?
I do not think thou canst, for then thou wast not   40
Out three years old.
    Miranda.   Certainly sir, I can.
    Prospero. By what? by any other house, or person?
Of any thing the image, tell me, that
Hath kept with thy remembrance.
    Miranda.   'Tis far off...
And rather like a dream, than an assurance
That my remembrance warrants...Had I not
Four—or five—women once, that tended me?

Prospero. Thou hadst; and more, Miranda: But how is it,
That this lives in thy mind? What seest thou else
50 In the dark backward and abysm of time?
If thou remembrest aught ere thou cam'st here,
How thou cam'st here thou mayst.
   Miranda.   But that I do not.
   Prospero. Twelve year since—Miranda—twelve year since,
Thy father was the Duke of Milan and
A prince of power...
   Miranda.   Sir, are not you my father?
   Prospero. Thy mother was a piece of virtue, and
She said thou wast my daughter; and thy father
Was Duke of Milan, and his only heir—
A princess; no worse issued.
   Miranda.   O the heavens,
60 What foul play had we, that we came from thence?
Or blessèd was't we did?
   Prospero.   Both, both, my girl....
By foul play—as thou sayst—were we heaved thence,
But blessedly holp hither.
   Miranda.   O my heart bleeds
To think o'th' teen that I have turned you to,
Which is from my remembrance. Please you, farther...
   Prospero. My brother, and thy uncle, called Antonio...
I pray thee mark me, that a brother should
Be so perfidious...he, whom next thyself
Of all the world I loved, and to him put
70 The manage of my state, as at that time
Through all the signories it was the first,
And Prospero, the prime duke, being so reputed
In dignity—and for the liberal arts,
Without a parallel; those being all my study,
The government I cast upon my brother,
And to my state grew stranger, being transported

And rapt in secret studies. Thy false uncle—
Dost thou attend me?

  Miranda [*recalling her eyes from the sea*]. Sir, most
    heedfully.

  Prospero. Being once perfected how to grant suits,
How to deny them: who t'advance, and who   80
To trash for over-topping; new created
The creatures that were mine, I say, or changed 'em,
Or else new formed 'em; having both the key
Of officer and office, set all hearts i'th' state
To what tune pleased his ear, that now he was
The ivy which had hid my princely trunk,
And sucked my verdure out on't: Thou attend'st not!

  Miranda [*guiltily*]. O good sir, I do.

   Prospero.   I pray thee mark me...
I thus neglecting worldly ends, all dedicated
To closeness, and the bettering of my mind   90
With that which, but by being so retired,
O'er-prized all popular rate, in my false brother
Awaked an evil nature; and my trust,
Like a good parent, did beget of him
A falsehood in its contrary, as great
As my trust was, which had indeed no limit,
A confidence sans bound....He, being thus lorded,
Not only with what my revénue yielded,
But what my power might else exact....like one,
†Who having minted truth by telling of it,
Made such a sinner of his memory,   100
To credit his own lie, he did believe
He was indeed the duke, out o'th' substitution
And executing th'outward face of royalty
With all prerogative: Hence his ambition growing...
Dost thou hear?

  Miranda.   Your tale, sir, would cure deafness.

Prospero. To have no screen between this part he played
And him he played it for, he needs will be
Absolute Milan—me (poor man) my library
110 Was dukedom large enough: of temporal royalties
He thinks me now incapable....confederates
(So dry he was for sway) wi' th' King of Naples
To give him annual tribute, do him homage,
Subject his 'coronet' to his 'crown,' and bend
The dukedom yet unbowed (alas, poor Milan!)
To most ignoble stooping.
    Miranda.   O the heavens!
    Prospero. Mark his condition, and th'event, then tell me,
If this might be a brother.
    Miranda.   I should sin
To think but nobly of my grandmother,
120 Good wombs have borne bad sons.
    Prospero.   Now the condition....
This King of Naples, being an enemy
To me inveterate, hearkens my brother's suit,
Which was, that he in lieu o'th' premises
Of homage, and I know not how much tribute,
Should presently extirpate me and mine
Out of the dukedom, and confer fair Milan,
With all the honours, on my brother: Whereon,
A treacherous army levied, one midnight,
Fated to th' purpose, did Antonio open
130 The gates of Milan, and i'th' dead of darkness
The ministers for th' purpose hurried thence
Me—and thy crying self.
    Miranda [*her tears falling again*]. Alack, for pity:
I not remembring how I cried out then
Will cry it o'er again: it is a hint
That wrings mine eyes to't.
    Prospero.   Hear a little further

And then I'll bring thee to the present business
Which now's upon's: without the which, this story
Were most impertinent.

Miranda.   Wherefore did they not
That hour destroy us?

Prospero.   Well demanded, wench:
My tale provokes that question. Dear, they durst not,   140
So dear the love my people bore me: nor set
A mark so bloody on the business; but
With colours fairer painted their foul ends....

                              [*he falters and proceeds swiftly*
In few, they hurried us aboard a bark,
Bore us some leagues to sea; where they prepared
A rotten carcass of a butt, not rigged,
Nor tackle, sail, nor mast, the very rats
Instinctively have quit it: There they hoist us
To cry to th' sea, that roared to us; to sigh
To th' winds, whose pity sighing back again   150
Did us but loving wrong.

Miranda.   Alack, what trouble
Was I then to you!

Prospero.   O, a cherubin
Thou wast that did preserve me; thou didst smile,
Infuséd with a fortitude from heaven—
When I have decked the sea with drops full salt,
Under my burden groaned—which raised in me
An undergoing stomach, to bear up
Against what should ensue.

Miranda.   How came we ashore?

Prospero. By Providence divine....
Some food we had, and some fresh water, that   160
A noble Neapolitan, Gonzalo,
Out of his charity, who being then appointed
Master of this design, did give us, with

Rich garments, linens, stuffs, and necessaries,
Which since have steaded much. So of his gentleness,
Knowing I loved my books, he furnished me
From mine own library with volumes that
I prize above my dukedom.
    Miranda.   Would I might
But ever see that man.
    Prospero.   Now I arise,
170 Sit still, and hear the last of our sea-sorrow...

                          [*he resumes his mantle*
Here in this island we arrived, and here
Have I, thy schoolmaster, made thee more profit
Than other princess' can, that have more time
For vainer hours—and tutors not so careful.
    Miranda. Heaven thank you for't....[*she kisses him*]
        And now I pray you sir—
For still 'tis beating in my mind—your reason
For raising this sea-storm?
    Prospero.   Know thus far forth.
By accident most strange, bountiful Fortune—
Now my dear lady—hath mine enemies
180 Brought to this shore: and by my prescience
I find my zenith doth depend upon
A most auspicious star, whose influence   > favourable,
If now I court not, but omit, my fortunes
Will ever after droop: Here cease more questions.
Thou art inclined to sleep... [*at a pass of his hands, her
eyes close and presently she sleeps*] 'tis a good dulness,
And give it way...I know thou canst not choose...

        He traces a magic circle on the grass

Come away, servant, come; I am ready now,
Approach my Ariel....[*he lifts his staff*] Come!

ARIEL appears aloft.

Ariel. All hail, great master, grave sir, hail: I come
To answer thy best pleasure; be't to fly,
To swim, to dive into the fire...to ride   190
On the curled clouds, [*alighting and bowing*] to thy
   strong bidding task
Ariel, and all his quality.
   Prospero.   Hast thou, spirit,
Performed to point the tempest that I bade thee?
   Ariel. To every article....
I boarded the king's ship: now on the beak,
Now in the waist, the deck, in every cabin,
I flamed amazement. Sometime I'ld divide
And burn in many places; on the topmast,
The yards and bowsprit, would I flame distinctly,   200
Then meet, and join; Jove's lightning, the precursors
O'th' dreadful thunder-claps, more momentary
And sight-outrunning were not; the fire and cracks
Of sulphurous roaring the most mighty Neptune
Seem to besiege, and make his bold waves tremble,
Yea, his dread trident shake.
   Prospero.   My brave spirit!
Who was so firm, so constant, that this coil
Would not infect his reason?
   Ariel.   Not a soul
But felt a fever of the mad, and played
Some tricks of desperation; all but mariners   210
Plunged in the foaming brine, and quit the vessel;
Then all afire with me the king's son Ferdinand,
With hair up-staring—then like reeds, not hair—
Was the first man that leaped; cried, 'Hell
   is empty,
And all the devils are here.'

Prospero.   Why, that's my spirit:
But was not this nigh shore?

Ariel.   Close by, my master.

Prospero. But are they, Ariel, safe?

Ariel.   Not a hair perished:
On their sustaining garments not a blemish,
But fresher than before: and, as thou bad'st me,

220 In troops I have dispersèd them 'bout the isle:
The king's son have I landed by himself,
Whom I left cooling of the air with sighs,
In an odd angle of the isle, and sitting,
His arms in this sad knot.   [*mimics*

Prospero.   Of the king's ship,
The mariners, say, how thou hast disposed,
And all the rest o'th' fleet?

Ariel.   Safely in harbour
Is the king's ship; in the deep nook, where once
Thou call'dst me up at midnight to fetch dew
From the still-vexed Bermoothes, there she's hid;

230 The mariners all under hatches stowed,
Who, with a charm joined to their suff'red labour,
I have left asleep: and for the rest o'th' fleet,
Which I dispersed, they all have met again,
And are upon the Mediterranean flote
Bound sadly home for Naples,
Supposing that they saw the king's ship wrecked,
And his great person perish.

Prospero.   Ariel, thy charge
Exactly is performed; but there's more work:
What is the time o'th' day?

Ariel.   Past the mid season,

240 *Prospero* [*glancing at the sun*]. At least two glasses...The
       time 'twixt six and now,
Must by us both be spent most preciously.

Ariel [*mutinous*]. Is there more toil? Since thou dost
    give me pains,
Let me remember thee what thou hast promised,
Which is not yet performed me.
  Prospero.   How now? moody?
What is't thou canst demand?
  Ariel.   My liberty.
  Prospero. Before the time be out? no more...
                                        [*lifting his staff*
  Ariel.   I prithee,
Remember I have done thee worthy service,
†Told thee no lies, made no mistakings, served
Without or grudge or grumblings; thou didst promise
To bate me a full year.
  Prospero.   Dost thou forget   250
From what a torment I did free thee?
  Ariel.   No.
  Prospero. Thou dost: and think'st it much to tread
    the ooze
Of the salt deep,
To run upon the sharp wind of the north,
To do me business in the veins o'th'earth
When it is baked with frost.
  Ariel.   I do not, sir.
  Prospero. Thou liest, malignant thing: hast thou forgot
The foul witch Sycorax, who with age and envy
Was grown into a hoop? hast thou forgot her?
  Ariel. No, sir.
  Prospero.   Thou hast. Where was she born? speak:
    tell me...   260
  Ariel. Sir, in Argier.
  Prospero.   O, was she so? I must
Once in a month recount what thou hast been,
Which thou forget'st.... This damned witch, Sycorax,

For mischiefs manifold, and sorceries terrible
To enter human hearing, from Argier
Thou know'st was banished: for one thing she did
They would not take her life...Is not this true?
   Ariel. Ay, sir.
   Prospero. This blue-eyed hag was hither brought
     with child,
270 And here was left by th' sailors; thou, my slave,
As thou report'st thyself, was then her servant,
And for thou wast a spirit too delicate
To act her earthy and abhorred commands,
Refusing her grand hests, she did confine thee,
By help of her more potent ministers,
And in her most unmitigable rage,
Into a cloven pine—within which rift
Imprisoned, thou didst painfully remain
A dozen years: within which space she died,
280 And left thee there: where thou didst vent thy groans,
As fast as mill-wheels strike: Then was this island,
(Save for the son that she did litter here,
A freckled whelp, hag-born) not honoured with
A human shape.
   Ariel.   Yes: Caliban her son.
   Prospero. Dull thing, I say so: he, that Caliban
Whom now I keep in service. Thou best know'st
What torment I did find thee in; thy groans
Did make wolves howl, and penetrate the breasts
Of ever-angry bears; it was a torment
290 To lay upon the damned, which Sycorax
Could not again undo: it was mine art,
When I arrived, and heard thee, that made gape
The pine, and let thee out.
   Ariel.   I thank thee master.
   Prospero. If thou more murmur'st, I will rend an oak,

And peg thee in his knotty entrails, till
Thou hast howled away twelve winters.

   Ariel.　　　　　　　　　　Pardon, master.
I will be correspondent to command,
And do my spriting gently.

   Prospero.　　　　　　　Do so: and after two days
I will discharge thee.

   Ariel.　　　　　That's my noble master!
What shall I do? say what? what shall I do?　　　　300

   Prospero. Go make thyself like a nymph o'th' sea,
     be subject
To no sight but thine and mine; invisible
To every eye-ball else: go take this shape,
And hither come in't...go...hence
With diligence.

       [Ariel vanishes. Prospero stoops over Miranda
Awake, dear heart, awake, thou hast slept well,
Awake.

   Miranda.　　　　The strangeness of your story put
Heaviness in me.

   Prospero.　　　　Shake it off...Come on,
We'll visit Caliban, my slave, who never
Yields us kind answer.　*[they approach a hole in the rock*

   Miranda.　　　　　'Tis a villain, sir,　　　　310
I do not love to look on.

   Prospero.　　　　　But, as 'tis,
We cannot miss him: he does make our fire,
Fetch in our wood, and serves in offices
That profit us...*[calling]* What ho! slave! Caliban!
Thou earth, thou! speak.

   Caliban [from the hole]. There's wood enough within.

   Prospero. Come forth, I say, there's other business
     for thee:
Come, thou tortoise, when?

ARIEL reappears, 'like a water-nymph.'

Fine apparition: my quaint Ariel,
Hark in thine ear. [*whispers*

   Ariel.   My lord, it shall be done.   [*vanishes*

320 *Prospero* [*to Caliban*]. Thou poisonous slave, got by the
      devil himself
Upon thy wicked dam; come forth.

CALIBAN comes from the hole, munching.

  Caliban. As wicked dew as e'er my mother brushed
With raven's feather from unwholesome fen
Drop on you both: a south-west blow on ye,
And blister you all o'er!

  Prospero. For this, be sure, to-night thou shalt
      have cramps,
Side-stitches that shall pen thy breath up—urchins
Shall, for that vast of night that they may work,
All exercise on thee: thou shalt be pinched
330 As thick as honeycomb, each pinch more stinging
†Than bees had made 'em.

   Caliban [*snarling*].   I must eat my dinner...
This island's mine, by Sycorax my mother,
Which thou tak'st from me: when thou cam'st first,
Thou strok'st me, and made much of me...wouldst
      give me
Water with berries in't; and teach me how
To name the bigger light, and how the less,
That burn by day and night: and then I loved thee,
And showed thee all the qualities o'th'isle,
The fresh springs, brine-pits, barren place and fertile.
340 Curst be I that did so! All the charms
Of Sycorax: toads, beetles, bats, light on you!
For I am all the subjects that you have,
Which first was mine own king: and here you sty me

In this hard rock, whiles you do keep from me
The rest o'th'island.

Prospero.　　　　　　　Thou most lying slave,
Whom stripes may move, not kindness: I have used thee—
Filth as thou art!—with human care, and lodged thee
In mine own cell, till thou didst seek to violate
The honour of my child.

Caliban. O ho, O ho! would't had been done!
Thou didst prevent me—I had peopled else
This isle with Calibans.

Miranda.　　　　　　　Abhorréd slave,
Which any print of goodness will not take,
Being capable of all ill: I pitied thee,
Took pains to make thee speak, taught thee each hour
One thing or other: when thou didst not—savage!—
Know thine own meaning, but wouldst gabble like
A thing most brutish, I endowed thy purposes
With words that made them known. But thy vile race,
Though thou didst learn, had that in't which
　　good natures　　　　　　　　　　　　　　　　　　360
Could not abide to be with; therefore wast thou
Deservedly confined into this rock,
Who hadst deserved more than a prison.

Caliban. You taught me language, and my profit on't
Is, I know how to curse: the red-plague rid you,
For learning me your language.

Prospero.　　　　　　　Hag-seed, hence...
Fetch us in fuel, and be quick thou'rt best
To answer other business: Shrug'st thou, malice?
If thou neglect'st, or dost unwillingly
What I command, I'll rack thee with old cramps,　　370
Fill all thy bones with achës, make thee roar,
That beasts shall tremble at thy din.

Caliban [*cowering*].　　　　　　　No, pray thee....

I must obey—his art is of such power, [*growls to himself*
It would control my dam's god Setebos,
And make a vassal of him.

   Prospero.   So, slave, hence!

          [*Caliban slinks away. Prospero and Mir-
           anda withdraw a little within the cave*

*Music heard: ARIEL 'invisible, playing and singing';
   FERDINAND following down the cliff path.*

ARIEL'S SONG.

    Come unto these yellow sands,
      And then take hands:
    Curtsied when you have, and kissed
      The wild waves whist:
380   Foot it featly here and there,
      And sweet sprites bear
        The burthen...Hark!
          Hark!
    '*Burthen dispersedly.*' Bow-wow!
    Ariel. The watch-dogs bark:
    Burthen. Bow-wow!
    Ariel. Hark, hark, I hear
    The strain of strutting chanticleer
      Cry—
390   *Burthen.* Cockadiddle-dow!

   Ferdinand. Where should this music be? i'th'air,
    or th'earth?
It sounds no more: and sure it waits upon
Some god o'th'island. Sitting on a bank,
Weeping again the king my father's wreck....
This music crept by me upon the waters,
Allaying both their fury and my passion
With its sweet air: thence I have followed it—

contrast between - Father & Son
+ Father + daughter

(he) has been over nurtured

(she) is of nature

Or it hath drawn me rather. But 'tis gone....
No, it begins again.

ARIEL'S SONG.

> Full fathom five thy father lies,   400
>   Of his bones are coral made:
> Those are pearls that were his eyes.
>   Nothing of him that doth fade,
> But doth suffer a sea-change
> Into something rich and strange...
> Sea-nymphs hourly ring his knell.
> *Burthen.* Ding-dong.
>   *Ariel.* Hark! now I hear them—
>   Ding-dong bell.

Ferdinand. The ditty does remember my drowned
   father.   410
This is no mortal business, nor no sound
That the earth owes: I hear it now above me.
  Prospero [*leading Miranda from the cave*]. The fringéd
   curtains of thine eye advance,
And say what thou seest yond.
  Miranda.   What is't? a spirit?
Lord, how it looks about...Believe me, sir,
It carries a brave form....But 'tis a spirit.
  Prospero. No wench, it eats and sleeps and hath
   such senses
As we have—such....This gallant which thou seest
Was in the wreck: and but he's something stained
With grief—that's beauty's canker [*touching her cheek*]
   —thou mightst call him   420
A goodly person: he hath lost his fellows,
And strays about to find 'em.
  Miranda [*moving forward, under the spell*]. I might
   call him
T.T.—5

A thing divine—for nothing natural
I ever saw so noble.
    Prospero [*holding back*]. It goes on I see,
As my soul prompts it...Spirit, fine spirit, I'll free thee
Within two days for this.
    Ferdinand [*as Miranda confronts him*]. Most sure,
        the goddess
On whom these airs attend...Vouchsafe my prayer
May know if you remain upon this island,
And that you will some good instruction give
430 How I may bear me here...My prime request,
Which I do last pronounce, is—O you wonder!—
If you be maid, or no?
    Miranda.   No wonder, sir,
But certainly a maid.
    Ferdinand.   My language? heavens...
I am the best of them that speak this speech,
Were I but where 'tis spoken.
    Prospero [*advancing*].   How? the best?
What wert thou if the King of Naples heard thee?
    Ferdinand. A single thing, as I am now, that wonders
To hear thee speak of Naples...He does hear me,
And that he does, I weep: myself am Naples,
440 Who with mine eyes—never since at ebb—beheld
The king my father wrecked.
    Miranda.   Alack, for mercy!
    Ferdinand. Yes, faith, and all his lords—the Duke of Milan
And his brave son being twain.
    Prospero [*to himself*].   The Duke of Milan
And his more braver daughter could control thee,
If now 'twere fit to do't...At the first sight
They have changed eyes...Delicate Ariel,
I'll set thee free for this....[*sternly*] A word, good sir.
I fear you have done yourself some wrong: a word.

Handwritten margin notes:
the things that she has produced the music
a snob
a snob
Prospero decides that ferdinand is too proud and needs bringing down.

Miranda. Why speaks my father so ungently? This
Is the third man that e'er I saw...the first,   450
That e'er I sighed for: pity move my father
To be inclined my way.
  Ferdinand.   O, if a virgin,
And your affection not gone forth, I'll make you
The queen of Naples.
  Prospero.   Soft, sir, one word more....
They are both in either's powers: but this swift business
I must uneasy make, lest too light winning
Make the prize light....One word more: I charge thee
That thou attend me: thou dost here usurp
The name thou ow'st not—and hast put thyself
Upon this island, as a spy, to win it   460
From me, the lord on't.
  Ferdinand.   No, as I am a man.
  Miranda. There's nothing ill can dwell in such
      a temple.
If the ill spirit have so fair a house,
Good things will strive to dwell with't.
  Prospero [*imperatively to Ferdinand*].   Follow me...
[*to Miranda*] Speak not you for him: he's a traitor...[*to
     Ferdinand*] Come,
I'll manacle thy neck and feet together:
Sea-water shalt thou drink: thy food shall be
The fresh-brook mussels, withered roots, and husks
Wherein the acorn cradled....Follow.
  Ferdinand.   No,
I will resist such entertainment, till   470
Mine enemy has more power.
            [*'he draws and is charmed from moving'*
  Miranda.   O dear father,
Make not too rash a trial of him, for
He's gentle, and not fearful.

Prospero. What, I say,
My foot my tutor! Put thy sword up traitor,
Who mak'st a show, but dar'st not strike, thy conscience
Is so possessed with guilt: come, from thy ward,
For I can here disarm thee with this stick,
And make thy weapon drop.

     [*Ferdinand's sword falls from his hand*
Miranda [*plucking his mantle*]. Beseech you father.
Prospero. Hence: hang not on my garments.
Miranda. Sir have pity,
480 I'll be his surety.

  Prospero. Silence: one word more
Shall make me chide thee, if not hate thee: what,
An advocate for an impostor! [*as she weeps*] Hush:
Thou think'st there is no more such shapes as he,
Having seen but him and Caliban...Foolish wench,
To th' most of men, this is a Caliban,
And they to him are angels.

  Miranda. My affections
Are then most humble: I have no ambition
To see a goodlier man.

  Prospero [*to Ferdinand*]. Come on, obey:
Thy nerves are in their infancy again,
490 And have no vigour in them.

  Ferdinand. So they are:
My spirits, as in a dream, are all bound up...
My father's loss, the weakness which I feel,
The wreck of all my friends, nor this man's threats,
To whom I am subdued, are but light to me,
Might I but through my prison once a day
Behold this maid: all corners else o'th'earth
Let liberty make use of...space enough
Have I in such a prison.

  Prospero. It works...[*to Ferdinand*] Come on....

[*to Ariel*] Thou hast done well, fine Ariel…[*to Ferdinand*]
    Follow me.
[*to Ariel*] Hark what thou else shalt do me.
  Miranda.   Be of comfort, 500
My father's of a better nature, sir,
Than he appears by speech: this is unwonted
Which now came from him.
  Prospero [*to Ariel*].   Thou shalt be as free
As mountain winds; but then exactly do
All points of my command.
  Ariel.   To th' syllable.
  Prospero [*turns again to Ferdinand*]. Come, follow:
    [*to Miranda*] speak not for him.

              They enter the cave.

    [2. 1.] *A forest glade in another part of the Island.*

*KING ALONSO lies upon the turf, his face buried in the
grass: GONZALO, ADRIAN, FRANCISCO, and others stand
about him: SEBASTIAN and ANTONIO converse apart in
low mocking tones.*

  Gonzalo. Beseech you, sir, be merry; you have cause,
So have we all, of joy; for our escape
Is much beyond our loss; our hint of woe
Is common—every day some sailor's wife,
The masters of some merchant, and the merchant,
Have just our theme of woe: But for the miracle—
I mean our preservation—few in millions
Can speak like us: then wisely, good sir, weigh
Our sorrow with our comfort.
  Alonso [*without looking up*]. Prithee, peace.
  Sebastian. He receives comfort like cold porridge. 10
  Antonio. The visitor will not give him o'er so.

[handwritten annotations:]
he can't cope with his situation.
→ always a counsellor or politician in every shakespeare play.
quite normal in Shakespeare day for men not to return for a voyage

Sebastian. Look, he's winding up the watch of his wit—
by and by it will strike.

Gonzalo. Sir—

Sebastian. One...tell.

Gonzalo. When every grief is entertained that's offered,
Comes to the entertainer—

Sebastian [*aloud*]. A dollar.

Gonzalo [*turning*]. Dolour comes to him, indeed. You
have spoken truer than you purposed.

20 *Sebastian.* You have taken it wiselier than I meant you
should.

Gonzalo [*to the king again*]. Therefore, my lord,—

Antonio. Fie, what a spendthrift is he of his tongue.

Alonso. I prithee, spare.

Gonzalo. Well, I have done: But yet—

Sebastian. He will be talking.

Antonio. Which, of he or Adrian, for a good wager,
first begins to crow?

Sebastian. The old cock.

30 *Antonio.* The cockerel.

Sebastian. Done: the wager?

Antonio. A laughter.

Sebastian. A match!

Adrian. Though this island seem to be desert,—

Antonio. Ha, ha, ha!

Sebastian. So! you're paid.

Adrian.—uninhabitable, and almost inaccessible,—

Sebastian. Yet—

Adrian.—yet—

40 *Antonio.* He could not miss't.

Adrian.—it must needs be of subtle, tender and delicate
temperance.

Antonio. 'Temperance' was a delicate wench.

Sebastian. Ay, and a subtle, as he most learnedly delivered.

Adrian. The air breathes upon us here most sweetly.

Sebastian. As if it had lungs, and rotten ones.

Antonio. Or, as 'twere perfumed by a fen.

Gonzalo. Here is every thing advantageous to life.

Antonio. True, save means to live.

Sebastian. Of that there's none, or little.

Gonzalo. How lush and lusty the grass looks! how green!

Antonio. The ground, indeed, is tawny.

Sebastian. With an eye of green in't.

Antonio. He misses not much.

Sebastian. No: he doth but mistake the truth totally.

Gonzalo. But the rarity of it is, which is indeed almost beyond credit,—

Sebastian. As many vouched rarities are.

Gonzalo.—that our garments, being, as they were, drenched in the sea, hold notwithstanding their freshness and glosses, being rather new dyed than stained with salt water.

Antonio. If but one of his pockets could speak, would it not say he lies?

Sebastian. Ay, or very falsely pocket up his report.

Gonzalo. Methinks our garments are now as fresh as when we put them on first in Afric, at the marriage of the king's fair daughter Claribel to the King of Tunis.

Sebastian. 'Twas a sweet marriage, and we prosper well in our return.

Adrian. Tunis was never graced before with such a paragon to their queen.

Gonzalo. Not since widow Dido's time.

Antonio. Widow? a pox o'that: How came that widow in? Widow Dido!

Sebastian. What if he had said 'widower Æneas' too?
Good Lord, how you take it!

80   *Adrian.* Widow Dido, said you? you make me study of
that: She was of Carthage, not of Tunis.

Gonzalo. This Tunis, sir, was Carthage.

Adrian. Carthage?

Gonzalo. I assure you, Carthage.

Antonio. His word is more than the miraculous harp.

Sebastian. He hath raised the wall, and houses too.

Antonio. What impossible matter will he make easy
next?

Sebastian. I think he will carry this island home in
90   his pocket, and give it his son for an apple.

Antonio. And, sowing the kernels of it in the sea,
bring forth more islands.

Gonzalo. Ay.

Antonio. Why, in good time.

Gonzalo. Sir, we were talking, that our garments seem
now as fresh as when we were at Tunis at the marriage
of your daughter, who is now queen.

Antonio. And the rarest that e'er came there.

Sebastian. Bate, I beseech you, widow Dido.

100   *Antonio.* O, widow Dido! ay, widow Dido.

Gonzalo. Is not, sir, my doublet as fresh as the first day
I wore it? I mean, in a sort.

Antonio. That sort was well fished for.

Gonzalo. When I wore it at your daughter's marriage?

Alonso [*sitting up*]. You cram these words into mine
    ears, against
The stomach of my sense...Would I had never
Married my daughter there: for, coming thence,
My son is lost, and, in my rate, she too,
Who is so far from Italy removed,
110 I ne'er again shall see her...O thou mine heir

Of Naples and of Milan, what strange fish
Hath made his meal on thee?
Francisco.   Sir, he may live.
I saw him beat the surges under him,
And ride upon their backs; he trod the water,
Whose enmity he flung aside, and breasted
The surge most swoln that met him: his bold head
'Bove the contentious waves he kept, and oared
Himself with his good arms in lusty stroke — *contrast with Ariel's*
To th' shore, that o'er his wave-worn basis bowed, *description*
As stooping to relieve him: I not doubt   120
He came alive to land.
    Alonso.   No, no, he's gone.
    Sebastian [aloud]. Sir, you may thank yourself for this   *cruel, a*
        great loss,   *political*
That would not bless our Europe with your daughter,   *message*
But rather loose her to an African,   *level*
Where she, at least, is banished from your eye,
Who hath cause to wet the grief on't.
    Alonso.   Prithee, peace.
    Sebastian. You were kneeled to, and importuned otherwise
By all of us: and the fair soul herself
Weighed between loathness and obedience, at
Which end o'th' beam sh'ould bow...We have lost
        your son,   130
I fear, for ever: Milan and Naples have
Moe widows in them of this business' making,
Than we bring men to comfort them:
The fault's your own.
    Alonso.   So is the dear'st o'th' loss.
    Gonzalo. My lord Sebastian,
The truth you speak doth lack some gentleness,
And time to speak it in: you rub the sore,
When you should bring the plaster.

(*Sebastian.*　　　　　　　　　　Very well.

(*Antonio.* And most chirurgeonly.

140　*Gonzalo.* It is foul weather in us all, good sir,
When you are cloudy.

(*Sebastian.*　　　　　　Fowl weather?

(*Antonio.*　　　　　　　　　　Very foul.

Gonzalo. Had I plantation of this isle, my lord,—

(*Antonio.* He'd sow't with nettle-seed.

(*Sebastian.*　　　　　　　　　Or docks, or mallows.

Gonzalo. And were the king on't, what would I do?

(*Sebastian.* 'Scape being drunk, for want of wine.

Gonzalo. I'th' commonwealth I would by contraries
Execute all things: for no kind of traffic
Would I admit: no name of magistrate:
Letters should not be known: riches, poverty,

150　And use of service—none: contract, succession,
Bourn, bound of land, tilth, vineyard—none:
No use of metal, corn, or wine, or oil:
No occupation, all men idle, all:
And women too, but innocent and pure:
No sovereignty—

(*Sebastian.*　　　　Yet he would be king on't.

(*Antonio.* The latter end of his commonwealth forgets
the beginning.

Gonzalo. All things in common nature should produce
Without sweat or endeavour: treason, felony,

160　Sword, pike, knife, gun, or need of any engine,
Would I not have: but nature should bring forth,
Of it own kind, all foison, all abundance,
To feed my innocent people.

(*Sebastian.* No marrying 'mong his subjects?

(*Antonio.* None, man, all idle; whores and knaves...

Gonzalo. I would with such perfection govern, sir,
T'excel the golden age, and—

(margin annotations in pencil:) Utopia

(handwritten note at bottom:) Speeches of Gonzalo's put in to flatter the Monarch — James I — Elizabeth + the Elector Palatinate. James wrote speeches on kingship.

Sebastian [*aloud*].   'Save his majesty!

Antonio. Long live Gonzalo!

Gonzalo.   Do you mark me, sir?

Alonso. Prithee, no more: thou dost talk nothing to me.

Gonzalo. I do well believe your highness, and did it to   170
minister occasion to these gentlemen, who are of such
sensible and nimble lungs, that they always use to laugh
at nothing.

Antonio. 'Twas you we laughed at.

Gonzalo. Who, in this kind of merry fooling, am nothing
to you: so you may continue, and laugh at nothing still.

Antonio. What a blow was there given!

Sebastian. An it had not fallen flat-long.

Gonzalo. You are gentlemen of brave mettle: you would
lift the moon out of her sphere—if she would continue in   180
it five weeks without changing!

> *ARIEL appears aloft, 'playing solemn music.'*

Sebastian. We would so, and then go a bat-fowling.

> *GONZALO turns away.*

Antonio. Nay, good my lord, be not angry.

Gonzalo. No, I warrant you. I will not adventure my
discretion so weakly...[*he lies down*] Will you laugh me
asleep, for I am very heavy?

Antonio. Go sleep, and hear us.

                    [*all sleep but Alonso, Sebastian and Antonio*

Alonso. What, all so soon asleep? I wish mine eyes
Would, with themselves, shut up my thoughts. I find,
They are inclined to do so.

Sebastian.   Please you, sir,   190
Do not omit the heavy offer of it:
It seldom visits sorrow; when it doth,
It is a comforter.

Antonio.   We two, my lord,
Will guard your person, while you take your rest,
And watch your safety.
Alonso.   Thank you...wondrous heavy.
                    [*Alonso sleeps. Ariel vanishes*
Sebastian. What a strange drowsiness possesses them!
Antonio. It is the quality o'th' climate.
Sebastian.   Why
Doth it not then our eyelids sink? I find not
Myself disposed to sleep.
Antonio.   Nor I. My spirits are nimble:
200 They fell together all, as by consent;
They dropped—as by a thunder-stroke...[*in a whisper,
          pointing at the sleepers*] What might,
Worthy Sebastian? O, what might? No more...
And yet, methinks, I see it in thy face,
What thou shouldst be: th'occasion speaks thee, and
My strong imagination sees a crown
Dropping upon thy head.
Sebastian.   What! art thou waking?
Antonio. Do you not hear me speak?
Sebastian.   I do, and surely
It is a sleepy language; and thou speak'st
Out of thy sleep: What is it thou didst say?
210 This is a strange repose, to be asleep
With eyes wide open; standing, speaking, moving...
And yet so fast asleep.
Antonio.   Noble Sebastian,
Thou let'st thy fortune sleep...die rather...wink'st
Whiles thou art waking.
Sebastian.   Thou dost snore distinctly,
There's meaning in thy snores.
Antonio. I am more serious than my custom: you
Must be so too, if heed me: which to do,

Trebles thee o'er.

   Sebastian.   Well: I am standing water.

   Antonio. I'll teach you how to flow.

   Sebastian.   Do so: to ebb

Hereditary sloth instructs me.

   Antonio.   O!   220

If you but knew how you the purpose cherish

Whiles thus you mock it: how, in stripping it,

You more invest it: ebbing men, indeed,—

Most often—do so near the bottom run

By their own fear, or sloth.

   Sebastian.   Prithee, say on.

The setting of thine eye and cheek proclaim

A matter from thee; and a birth, indeed,

Which throes thee much to yield.

   Antonio [*points to Gonzalo*].   Thus, sir:

Although this lord of weak remembrance; this,

Who shall be of as little memory   230

When he is earthed, hath here almost persuaded—

For he's a spirit of persuasion, only

Professes to persuade—the king his son's alive,

'Tis as impossible that he's undrowned,

As he that sleeps here swims.

   Sebastian.   I have no hope

That he's undrowned.

   Antonio.   O, out of that 'no hope'

What great hope have you! no hope, that way, is

Another way so high an hope, that even

Ambition cannot pierce a wink beyond,

But doubt discovery there. Will you grant with me   240

That Ferdinand is drowned?

   Sebastian.   He's gone.

   Antonio.   Then, tell me,

Who's the next heir of Naples?

Sebastian.   Claribel.

Antonio. She that is queen of Tunis: she that dwells
Ten leagues beyond man's life: she that from Naples
Can have no note—unless the sun were post:
The man i'th' moon's too slow—till new-born chins
Be rough and razorable: she that...from whom
We were all sea-swallowed, though some cast again,
†And that by destiny—to perform an act,
250 Whereof what's past is prologue; what to come,
In yours and my discharge.

   Sebastian.   What stuff is this? How say you?
'Tis true, my brother's daughter's queen of Tunis,
So is she heir of Naples—'twixt which regions
There is some space.

   Antonio.   A space whose every cubit
Seems to cry out, 'How shall that Claribel
Measure us back to Naples? Keep in Tunis,
And let Sebastian wake'....Say, this were death
That now hath seized them—why, they were no worse
Than now they are: There be that can rule Naples,
260 As well as he that sleeps: lords, that can prate
As amply and unnecessarily
As this Gonzalo: I myself could make
A chough of as deep chat: O, that you bore
The mind that I do; what a sleep were this
For your advancement! Do you understand me?

   Sebastian. Methinks I do.

   Antonio.   And how does your content
Tender your own good fortune?

   Sebastian.   I remember
You did supplant your brother Prospero.

   Antonio.   True:
And look how well my garments sit upon me,
270 Much feater than before: my brother's servants

Were then my fellows, now they are my men.
  Sebastian. But, for your conscience?
  Antonio. Ay, sir: where lies that? if 'twere a kibe,
'Twould put me to my slipper: but I feel not
This deity in my bosom...Twenty consciences,
That stand 'twixt me and Milan, candied be they,
And melt ere they molest...Here lies your brother,
No better than the earth he lies upon.
If he were that which now he's like—[*sinks his voice*]
      that's dead—
Whom I with this obedient steel—[*touching his dagger*]
      three inches of it—   280
Can lay to bed for ever...whiles you, doing thus,
To the perpetual wink for aye might put
This ancient morsel...[*pointing to Gonzalo*] this Sir
      Prudence, who
Should not upbraid our course...For all the rest,
They'll take suggestion, as a cat laps milk—
They'll tell the clock to any business that
We say befits the hour.
  Sebastian.   Thy case, dear friend,
Shall be my precedent: as thou got'st Milan,
I'll come by Naples...Draw thy sword. One stroke
Shall free thee from the tribute which thou payest,   290
And I the king shall love thee.
  Antonio.   Draw together:
                          [*they unsheath swords*
And when I rear my hand, do you the like
To fall it on Gonzalo.
  Sebastian.   O, but one word.
                              [*they talk apart*

'Music.' ARIEL *appears again, unseen by them,*
and bends over GONZALO.

Ariel. My master through his art foresees the danger,
That you—his friend—are in, and sends me forth,
(For else his project dies) to keep them living.

[*'sings in Gonzalo's ear'*

While you here do snoring lie,
Open-eyed conspiracy
His time doth take:
300   If of life you keep a care,
Shake off slumber, and beware,....
Awake! Awake!

Antonio. Then let us both be sudden.

†*Gonzalo* [*waking*]. Now, good angels preserve
   the king!
Why, how now? Ho! awake! [*shaking Alonso,*
  who wakes.

Alonso [*to Antonio and Sebastian*]. Why are you drawn?
Wherefore this ghastly looking? What's the matter?

Sebastian. Whiles we stood here securing your repose,
Even now, we heard a hollow burst of bellowing
Like bulls, or rather lions—did't not wake you?
310 It struck mine ear most terribly.

Alonso.   I heard nothing.

Antonio. O, 'twas a din to fright a monster's ear;
To make an earthquake! sure, it was the roar
Of a whole herd of lions.

Alonso.   Heard you this, Gonzalo?

Gonzalo. Upon mine honour, sir, I heard a humming—
And that a strange one too—which did awake me...
I shaked you, sir, and cried: as mine eyes opened,
I saw their weapons drawn...there was a noise,
†That's verity. 'Tis best we stand upon our guard;

Or that we quit this place: let's draw our weapons.
  Alonso. Lead off this ground, and let's make
     further search   320
For my poor son.
  Gonzalo.   Heavens keep him from these beasts...
For he is, sure, i'th'island.
  Alonso.   Lead away.
  Ariel [*as the band moves off*]. Prospero my lord shall
    know what I have done....
So, king, go safely on to seek thy son.   [*vanishes*

    [2. 2.] *A barren upland: the weather lowering.*
     '*Enter* CALIBAN, *with a burden of wood.*
       A noise of thunder heard.'

  Caliban. All the infections that the sun sucks up
From bogs, fens, flats, on Prosper fall, and make him
By inch-meal a disease: [*lightning*] His spirits hear me,
And yet I needs must curse....[*casts down his burden*]
    But they'll nor pinch,
Fright me with urchin-shows, pitch me i'th' mire,
Nor lead me, like a firebrand, in the dark
Out of my way, unless he bid 'em; but
For every trifle are they set upon me—
Sometime like apes, that mow and chatter at me,
And after bite me: then like hedgehogs which   10
Lie tumbling in my barefoot way, and mount
Their pricks at my footfall: sometime am I
All wound with adders, who with cloven tongues
Do hiss me into madness...

        Enter TRINCULO.
            Lo, now, lo!
Here comes a spirit of his—and to torment me,

For bringing wood in slowly: I'll fall flat—
Perchance he will not mind me.

    [*he falls upon his face, so that his gaberdine hides him*
Trinculo [*stumbling forward, looking at the sky*]. Here's
neither bush nor shrub, to bear off any weather at all...
and another storm brewing, I hear it sing i'th' wind:
yond same black cloud, yond huge one, looks like a foul
bombard that would shed his liquor: if it should thunder,
as it did before, I know not where to hide my head: yond
same cloud cannot choose but fall by pailfuls.:...[*trips over*
Caliban] What have we here? a man or a fish? dead or
alive? [*sniffing*] A fish, he smells like a fish...a very ancient
and fish-like smell...a kind of not-of-the-newest poor-
john: a strange fish...Were I in England now, as once
I was, and had but this fish painted,—not a holiday
fool there but would give a. piece of silver: there
would this monster make a man: any strange beast
there makes a man: when they will not give a doit to
relieve a lame beggar, they will lay out ten to see a dead
Indian...[*lifts the gaberdine*] Legged like a man; and his
fins like arms...[*feels the body warily*] Warm, o' my
troth! [*starts back*] I do now let loose my opinion; hold
it no longer; this is no fish, but an islander, that hath
lately suffered by a thunderbolt: [*more thunder*] Alas!
the storm is come again: my best way is to creep under
his gaberdine: [*he does so, at the tail end*] there is no
other shelter hereabout: misery acquaints a man with
strange bed-fellows: [*pulling the skirt round him*] I will
here shroud till the dregs of the storm be past.

    '*Enter* STEPHANO, *singing*'; *a bottle in his hand*.

    Stephano. I shall no more to sea, to sea,
             Here shall I die ashore,—
This is a very scurvy tune to sing at a man's funeral:

Well, here's my comfort.   ['*drinks*'

['*sings*'] The master, the swabber, the bos'n, and I,
    The gunner, and his mate,
  Loved Mall, Meg, and Marian, and Margery,   50
     But none of us cared for Kate....
     For she had a tongue with a tang,
     Would cry to a sailor, 'Go hang':
  She loved not the savour of tar nor of pitch,
  Yet a tailor might scratch her where'er she did itch....
     Then to sea, boys, and let her go hang.

This is a scurvy tune too: but here's my comfort. ['*drinks*'

Caliban. Do not torment me...O!

Stephano. What's the matter? [*turning*] Have we devils
here? Do you put tricks upon's with savages and men   60
of Ind, ha? I have not 'scaped drowning, to be afeard
now of your four legs: for it hath been said; As proper a
man as ever went on four legs cannot make him give
ground: and it shall be said so again, while Stephano
breathes at' nostrils.

Caliban. The spirit torments me...O!

Stephano. This is some monster of the isle, with four
legs; who hath got, as I take it, an ague...Where the devil
should he learn our language? I will give him some relief,
if it be but for that...If I can recover him, and keep him   70
tame, and get to Naples with him, he's a present for
any emperor that ever trod on neat's-leather.

Caliban [*showing his face*]. Do not torment me, prithee:
I'll bring my wood home faster.

Stephano. He's in his fit now; and does not talk after
the wisest; he shall taste of my bottle: if he have never
drunk wine afore, it will go near to remove his fit: if I
can recover him, and keep him tame, I will not take too
much for him; he shall pay for him that hath him, and
that soundly.   [*seizing him by the shoulder* 80

Caliban. Thou dost me yet but little hurt;
Thou wilt anon, I know it by thy trembling:
Now Prosper works upon thee.

Stephano. Come on your ways: [*thrusting the bottle in
his face*] open your mouth: here is that which will
give language to you, cat; open your mouth; this will
shake your shaking, I can tell you, and that soundly...
[*Caliban drinks*] you cannot tell who's your friend; open
your chaps again.

90 *Trinculo.* I should know that voice: It should be—but
he is drowned; and these are devils; O, defend me!

aspirit

Stephano. Four legs and two voices; a most delicate
monster...His forward voice now is to speak well of his
friend; his backward voice is to utter foul speeches, and
to detract: If all the wine in my bottle will recover him,
I will help his ague: Come...[*Caliban drinks again*]
Amen, I will pour some in thy other mouth.

Trinculo. Stephano,—

Stephano [*starting back*]. Doth thy other mouth call
100 me? Mercy, mercy! This is a devil, and no monster:
I will leave him—I have no long spoon.

Trinculo. Stephano...if thou beest Stephano, touch me,
and speak to me: for I am Trinculo; be not afeard—thy
good friend Trinculo.

Stephano. If thou beest Trinculo...[*returns*] come forth:
[*grips his ankles*] I'll pull thee by the lesser legs: [*pulls
and pauses*] if any be Trinculo's legs, these are they:
[*spies his face*] Thou art very Trinculo, indeed: How
cam'st thou to be the siege of this moon-calf? Can he
110 vent Trinculos?

lunatic

Trinculo [*staggering to his feet*]. I took him to be killed
with a thunder-stroke...But art thou not drowned, Stephano? I hope now, thou art not drowned: Is the storm
overblown? I hid me under the dead moon-calf's gaber-

Trinculo afraid that he is a spirit &
Stephano too

dine, for fear of the storm: [*fondling him foolishly*] And
art thou living, Stephano? O Stephano, two Neapolitans
'scaped!

Stephano. Prithee do not turn me about, my stomach
is not constant.

Caliban. These be fine things, an if they be not sprites: 120
That's a brave god, and bears celestial liquor:
I will kneel to him.   [*he does so*

Stephano. How didst thou 'scape? How cam'st thou
hither? Swear by this bottle, how thou cam'st hither...
I escaped upon a butt of sack, which the sailors heaved
o'er-board—by this bottle! which I made of the bark of
a tree, with mine own hands, since I was cast ashore.

Caliban [*coming forward*]. I'll swear upon that bottle,
to be thy true subject, for the liquor is not earthly.

Stephano. Here: [*offering Trinculo the bottle*] swear then 130
how thou escapedst.

Trinculo. Swam ashore, man, like a duck...I can swim
like a duck, I'll be sworn.

Stephano. Here, kiss the book....[*Trinculo drinks*]
Though thou canst swim like a duck, thou art made like
a goose [*snatching the bottle from him*].

Trinculo. O Stephano, hast any more of this?

Stephano. The whole butt, man. My cellar is in a rock
by th' sea-side, where my wine is hid...[*spies Caliban*]
How now, moon-calf? how does thine ague?   140

Caliban. Hast thou not dropped from heaven?

Stephano. Out o'th' moon, I do assure thee....[*draining
the bottle*] I was the man i'th' moon, when time was.

Caliban [*bowing low*]. I have seen thee in her: and I
    do adore thee:
My mistress showed me thee, and thy dog, and thy bush.

Stephano. Come, swear to that: kiss the book...I will
furnish it anon with new 'contents'. Swear.

T.T.—6

Trinculo. By this good light, this is a very shallow monster: I afeard of him? a very weak monster...The man i' th' moon! a most poor credulous monster...[*as Caliban sucks at the empty bottle*] Well drawn, monster, in good sooth.

Caliban. I'll show thee every fertile inch of the island: And I will kiss thy foot: I prithee be my god.

Trinculo. By this light, a most perfidious and drunken monster. When's god's asleep, he'll rob his bottle.

Caliban. I'll kiss thy foot, I'll swear myself thy subject.

Stephano. Come on then: down, and swear.

[*Caliban kneels with his back to Trinculo*

Trinculo. I shall laugh myself to death at this puppy-headed monster: a most scurvy monster: I could find in my heart to beat him—

Stephano. Come, kiss. [*Caliban kisses his foot*

Trinculo. —but that the poor monster's in drink...An abominable monster!

Caliban. I'll show thee the best springs: I'll pluck
    thee berries:
I'll fish for thee, and get thee wood enough....
A plague upon the tyrant that I serve;
I'll bear him no more sticks, but follow thee,
Thou wondrous man.

Trinculo. A most ridiculous monster, to make a wonder of a poor drunkard!

Caliban. I prithee, let me bring thee where crabs grow;
And I with my long nails will dig thee pig-nuts;
Show thee a jay's nest, and instruct thee how
To snare the nimble marmozet: I'll bring thee
To clustring filberts, and sometimes I'll get thee
†Young scamels from the rock: Wilt thou go with me?

Stephano. I prithee now, lead the way, without any more talking....Trinculo, the king and all our company

else being drowned, we will inherit here: [*to Caliban*] 180
Here; bear my bottle: [*clutching at Trinculo's arm*] Fellow
Trinculo; we'll fill him by and by again.

   Caliban ['*sings drunkenly*']. Farewell master; farewell,
     farewell.
   Trinculo. A howling monster: a drunken monster.
   Caliban. No more dams I'll make for fish,
           Nor fetch in firing
           At requiring,
        Nor scrape trenchering, nor wash dish,
         'Ban 'Ban, Ca-Caliban
         Has a new master—get a new man.   190
Freedom, high-day! high-day, freedom! freedom, high-
    day, freedom!
   Stephano. O brave monster; lead the way. [*they reel off*

[3. 1.] *Before Prospero's cell:* '*FERDINAND, bearing a log.*'

   Ferdinand. There be some sports are painful; and
     their labour
Delight in them sets off: some kinds of baseness
Are nobly undergone; and most poor matters
Point to rich ends...This my mean task
Would be as heavy to me as odious, but
The mistress which I serve quickens what's dead,
And makes my labours—pleasures...O, she is
Ten times more gentle than her father's crabbed;
And he's composed of harshness....[*he sits*] I must remove
Some thousands of these logs, and pile them up,   10
Upon a sore injunction; my sweet mistress
Weeps, when she sees me work, and says, such baseness
Had never like executor...[*rising to continue*] I forget...
But these sweet thoughts do even refresh my labours—
†Most busie lest, when I doe it.

MIRANDA comes from the cave; PROSPERO, behind her,
stands at the door, unseen.

Miranda.   Alas, now pray you,
Work not so hard: I would the lightning had
Burnt up those logs that you are enjoined to pile:
Pray, set it down, and rest you: when this burns,
'Twill weep for having wearied you...My father
20 Is hard at study; pray now, rest yourself—
He's safe for these three hours.
 Ferdinand.   O most dear mistress,
The sun will set before I shall discharge
What I must strive to do.
 Miranda.   If you'll sit down,
I'll bear your logs the while: pray give me that,
I'll carry it to the pile.
 Ferdinand.   No, precious creature,—
I had rather crack my sinews, break my back,
Than you should such dishonour undergo,
While I sit lazy by.
 Miranda.   It would become me
As well as it does you; and I should do it
30 With much more ease: for my good will is to it,
And yours it is against.
 (*Prospero.*   Poor worm thou art infected,
This visitation shows it.
 Miranda.   You look wearily.
 Ferdinand. No, noble mistress, 'tis fresh morning
  with me
When you are by at night: I do beseech you—
Chiefly that I might set it in my prayers—
What is your name?
 Miranda.   Miranda,—O my father,
I have broke your hest to say so!

Ferdinand.　　　　　　　　　Admired Miranda!
Indeed the top of admiration, worth
What's dearest to the world! Full many a lady
I have eyed with best regard, and many a time 　　40
Th' harmony of their tongues hath into bondage
Brought my too diligent ear: for several virtues
Have I liked several women—never any
With so full soul, but some defect in her
Did quarrel with the noblest grace she owed,
And put it to the foil....But you, O you,
So perfect, and so peerless, are created
Of every creature's best.
Miranda.　　　　　　　I do not know
One of my sex; no woman's face remember,
Save, from my glass, mine own: nor have I seen 　　50
More that I may call men than you, good friend,
And my dear father: how features are abroad,
I am skilless of; but, by my modesty—　　*[faltering*
The jewel in my dower—I would not wish
Any companion in the world but you;
Nor can imagination form a shape,
Besides yourself, to like of...But I prattle
Something too wildly, and my father's precepts
I therein do forget.
Ferdinand.　　　　　I am, in my condition,
A prince, Miranda—I do think, a king, 　　60
(I would not so!) and would no more endure
This wooden slavery, than to suffer
The flesh-fly blow my mouth...Hear my soul speak....
The very instant that I saw you, did
My heart fly to your service, there resides
To make me slave to it, and for your sake
Am I this patient log-man.
Miranda.　　　　　　　Do you love me?

Ferdinand. O heaven, O earth, bear witness to
　　　this sound,
And crown what I profess with kind event
70　If I speak true...if hollowly, invert
What best is boded me to mischief...I,
Beyond all limit of what else i'th' world,
Do love, prize, honour you.
　　Miranda.　　　　　　　　　　I am a fool
To weep at what I am glad of.
　　(*Prospero.*　　　　　　　　Fair encounter
Of two most rare affections: heavens rain grace
On that which breeds between 'em!
　　Ferdinand.　　　　　　　　　Wherefore weep you?
　　Miranda. At mine unworthiness, that dare not offer
What I desire to give; and much less take
What I shall die to want...But this is trifling—
80　And all the more it seeks to hide itself,
The bigger bulk it shows....Hence bashful cunning,
And prompt me plain and holy innocence....
I am your wife, if you will marry me;
If not, I'll die your maid: to be your fellow
You may deny me, but I'll be your servant,
Whether you will or no.
　　Ferdinand [*kneeling*].　　My mistress,—dearest!
And I thus humble ever.
　　Miranda.　　　　　　　　　My husband then?
　　Ferdinand. Ay, with a heart as willing
As bondage e'er of freedom: here's my hand.
90　*Miranda.* And mine, with my heart in't; and now
　　　farewell
Till half an hour hence.
　　Ferdinand.　　　　　　A thousand! thousand!
　　　　　　[*Miranda pursues her way: Ferdinand goes to fetch
　　　　　　　　　　　　　　　　　more logs*

R + O

Prospero. So glad of this as they I cannot be,
Who are surprised with all; but my rejoicing
At nothing can be more. I'll to my book,
For yet, ere supper time, must I perform
Much business appertaining.   [*he turns back into his cell*

[3.2.] *A cove by the sea: on one side the land slopes gently down to the shore, on the other are cliffs with a little cave.* STEPHANO, TRINCULO *and* CALIBAN *sit by the entrance to the cave, drinking.*

Stephano. Tell not me—when the butt is out we will drink water, not a drop before; therefore bear up, and board 'em. Servant-monster, drink to me.

Trinculo. Servant-monster! [*pledges Stephano*] †The Sophy of this island! They say there's but five upon this isle; we are three of them—if th'other two be brained like us, the state totters.

Stephano. Drink servant-monster when I bid thee. Thy eyes are almost set in thy head.

Trinculo. Where should they be set else? he were a   10
brave monster indeed, if they were set in his tail.

Stephano. My man-monster hath drowned his tongue in sack: for my part, the sea cannot drown me—I swam, ere I could recover the shore, five-and-thirty leagues, off and on. By this light thou shalt be my lieutenant, monster, or my standard.

Trinculo. Your lieutenant if you list—he's no standard.

Stephano. We'll not run, Monsieur Monster.

Trinculo. Nor go neither: but you'll lie, like dogs, and
yet say nothing neither.   20

Stephano. Moon-calf, speak once in thy life, if thou beest a good moon-calf.

Caliban. How does thy honour? Let me lick thy shoe: I'll not serve him, he is not valiant.

Trinculo. Thou liest, most ignorant monster, I am in case to justle a constable: Why, thou debauched fish thou, was there ever a man a coward, that hath drunk so much sack as I to-day? Wilt thou tell a monstrous lie, being but half a fish, and half a monster?

30 *Caliban.* Lo how he mocks me! wilt thou let him, my lord?

Trinculo. 'Lord,' quoth he! that a monster should be such a natural!

Caliban. Lo, lo, again! bite him to death, I prithee.

Stephano. Trinculo, keep a good tongue in your head: if you prove a mutineer,—the next tree! The poor monster's my subject, and he shall not suffer indignity.

Caliban. I thank my noble lord....Wilt thou be pleased To hearken once again to the suit I made to thee?

40 *Stephano.* Marry will I: kneel and repeat it. I will stand, and so shall Trinculo.

[*Caliban kneels, Stephano and Trinculo totter to their feet*

'*Enter Ariel, invisible.*'

Caliban. As I told thee before, I am subject to a tyrant— A sorcerer, that by his cunning hath Cheated me of the island.

Ariel.   Thou liest.

Caliban [*turning on Trinculo*]. Thou liest, thou jesting monkey, thou:

I would, my valiant master would destroy thee.... I do not lie.

Stephano. Trinculo, if you trouble him any more in's tale, by this hand, I will supplant some of your teeth.

50 *Trinculo.* Why, I said nothing.

Stephano. Mum then, and no more: [*to Caliban*]Proceed.

Caliban. I say, by sorcery, he got this isle— From me he got it. If thy greatness will

Revenge it on him—for I know thou dar'st,
But this thing dare not—
  Stephano.   That's most certain.
  Caliban. Thou shalt be lord of it, and I will serve thee.
  Stephano. How now shall this be compassed? Canst
thou bring me to the party?
  Caliban. Yea, yea, my lord, I'll yield him thee asleep,
Where thou mayst knock a nail into his head.   60
  Ariel. Thou liest, thou canst not.
  Caliban. What a pied ninny's this! Thou scurvy patch!
I do beseech thy greatness, give him blows,
And take his bottle from him: when that's gone,
He shall drink nought but brine, for I'll not show **him**
Where the quick freshes are.
  Stephano. Trinculo, run into no further danger: inter-
rupt the monster one word further, and, by this hand,
I'll turn my mercy out of doors, and make a stock-fish
of thee.   70
  Trinculo. Why, what did I? I did nothing: I'll go
further off.
  Stephano. Didst thou not say he lied?
  Ariel. Thou liest.
  Stephano. Do I so? take thou that [*strikes him*]. As you
like this, give me the lie another time.
  Trinculo. I did not give the lie: Out of your wits, and
      hearing too?
A pox o'your bottle! this can sack, and drinking do:
a murrain on your monster, and the devil take your
fingers!   80
  Caliban. Ha, ha, ha!
  Stephano. Now, forward with your tale...
Prithee stand further off.   [*threatening Trinculo*
  Caliban. Beat him enough: after a little time,
I'll beat him too.

Stephano.   Stand further: Come, proceed.

Caliban. Why, as I told thee, 'tis a custom
with him
I'th'afternoon to sleep: there thou mayst brain him,
Having first seized his books: or with a log
Batter his skull, or paunch him with a stake,
90 Or cut his wezand with thy knife....Remember,
First to possess his books; for without them
He's but a sot, as I am; nor hath not
One spirit to command: they all do hate him,
As rootedly as I. Burn but his books.
He has brave utensils—for so he calls them—
Which, when he has a house, he'll deck withal.
And that most deeply to consider, is
The beauty of his daughter....he himself
Calls her a nonpareil: I never saw a woman,
100 But only Sycorax my dam and she;
But she as far surpasseth Sycorax,
As great'st does least.

Stephano.   Is it so brave a lass?

Caliban. Ay lord, she will become thy bed, I warrant,
And bring thee forth brave brood.

Stephano. Monster, I will kill this man: his daughter
and I will be king and queen—save our graces!—and
Trinculo and thyself shall be viceroys...
Dost thou like the plot, Trinculo?

Trinculo. Excellent.

110 *Stephano.* Give me thy hand—I am sorry I beat thee:
but, while thou liv'st, keep a good tongue in thy head.

Caliban. Within this half hour will he be asleep.
Wilt thou destroy him then?

Stephano.   Ay, on mine honour.

Ariel. This will I tell my master.

Caliban. Thou mak'st me merry: I am full of pleasure,

Let us be jocund....Will you troll the catch
You taught me but while-ere?

Stephano. At thy request, monster, I will do reason, any
reason: Come on, Trinculo, let us sing.   ['*sings*'
  Flout 'em, and cout 'em: and scout 'em, and flout 'em,   120
  Thought is free.

Caliban. That's not the tune.

        '*ARIEL plays the tune on a tabor and pipe.*'

Stephano. What is this same?

Trinculo [*staring about him*]. This is the tune of our
catch, played by the picture of Nobody.

Stephano [*shakes his fist*]. If thou beest a man, show thyself in thy likeness: if thou beest a devil, take 't as thou list.

Trinculo [*maudlin*]. O forgive me my sins!

Stephano. He that dies, pays all debts: I defy thee; [*his
courage suddenly ebbing*] Mercy upon us!   130

Caliban. Art thou afeard?

Stephano. No, monster, not I.

Caliban. Be not afeard—the isle is full of noises,
Sounds and sweet airs, that give delight and hurt not:
Sometimes a thousand twangling instruments
Will hum about mine ears; and sometime voices,
That, if I then had waked after long sleep,
Will make me sleep again—and then, in dreaming,
The clouds methought would open, and show riches
Ready to drop upon me, that when I waked   140
I cried to dream again.

Stephano. This will prove a brave kingdom to me, where
I shall have my music for nothing.

Caliban. When Prospero is destroyed.

Stephano. That shall be by and by: I remember the story.

Trinculo. The sound is going away. Let 's follow it, and
after do our work.

Stephano. Lead monster, we'll follow: I would I could see this taborer—he lays it on.

150   *Trinculo.* Wilt come? I'll follow, Stephano.

                  [they follow Ariel up the cove

[3. 3.] *The lime-grove above Prospero's cave, close to the summit of the cliff.* ALONSO *and his train, tired and dejected, wend their way through the trees;* GONZALO *lags behind.*

  Gonzalo. By'r lakin, I can go no further, sir.
My old bones ache: here's a maze trod, indeed,
Through forth-rights and meanders: by your patience,
I needs must rest me.

  Alonso.   Old lord, I cannot blame thee,
Who am myself attached with weariness,
To th' dulling of my spirits: sit down, and rest...

    [Alonso, Gonzalo, Adrian and Francisco seat themselves
Even here I will put off my hope, and keep it
No longer for my flatterer: he is drowned
Whom thus we stray to find, and the sea mocks
10 Our frustrate search on land...well, let him go.

  Antonio [standing, with Sebastian, apart from the rest].
I am right glad that he's so out of hope:
Do not, for one repulse, forego the purpose
That you resolved t'effect.

  Sebastian.   The next advantage
Will we take throughly.

  Antonio.   Let it be to-night,
For, now they are oppressed with travel, they
Will not, nor cannot, use such vigilance
As when they are fresh.

  Sebastian.   I say, to-night: no more.

'*Solemn and strange music: and* PROSPER *on the top,
invisible.*'

Alonso. What harmony is this? my good friends, hark!
Gonzalo. Marvellous sweet music!

'*Enter several strange shapes, bringing in a banquet; and
dance about it with gentle actions of salutation; and, in-
viting the king, &c. to eat, they depart.*'

Alonso. Give us kind keepers, heavens: what were these?　20
Sebastian. A living drollery: now I will believe
That there are unicorns: that in Arabia
There is one tree, the phœnix' throne, one phœnix
At this hour reigning there.
Antonio.　　　　　　　　I'll believe both:
And what does else want credit, come to me,
And I'll be sworn 'tis true: travellers ne'er did lie,
Though fools at home condemn 'em.
Gonzalo.　　　　　　　　If in Naples
I should report this now, would they believe me?
If I should say, I saw such islanders,—
For, certes, these are people of the island,　　　　30
Who, though they are of monstrous shape, yet note
Their manners are more gentle-kind, than of
Our human generation you shall find
Many, nay, almost any.
(Prospero.　　　　　　　Honest lord,
Thou hast said well: for some of you there present...
Are worse than devils.
Alonso.　　　　　　I cannot too much muse
Such shapes, such gesture, and such sound, expressing—
Although they want the use of tongue—a kind
Of excellent dumb discourse.
(Prospero [smiling grimly].　　Praise in departing.

40 *Francisco.* They vanished strangely.

Sebastian. No matter, since
They have left their viands behind; for we have
    stomachs....

> [*Sebastian surveys the banquet hungrily*

Will't please you taste of what is here?

Alonso. Not I.

Gonzalo. Faith, sir, you need not fear. When we
    were boys,
Who would believe that there were mountaineers,
Dew-lapped like bulls, whose throats had hanging at 'em
Wallets of flesh? or that there were such men
Whose heads stood in their breasts? which now we find
Each putter-out of five for one will bring us
Good warrant of.

Alonso. I will stand to, and feed,
50 Although my last—no matter, since I feel
The best is past...Brother: my lord the duke,
Stand to and do as we.

> [*Alonso, Sebastian and Antonio seat themselves*

'*Thunder and lightning. Enter* ARIEL *like a harpy; claps
his wings upon the table, and, with a quaint device, the
banquet vanishes.*'

Ariel. You are three men of sin, whom destiny,
That hath to instrument this lower world
And what is in't, the never-surfeited sea
Hath caused to belch up you; and on this island,
Where man doth not inhabit, you 'mongst men
Being most unfit to live. [*the three draw their swords*]
    I have made you mad;
And even with such-like valour men hang and drown
60 Their proper selves: [*they make to attack, but are charmed
    from moving*] You fools! I and my fellows

Are ministers of fate. The elements,
Of whom your swords are tempered, may as well
Wound the loud winds, or with bemocked-at stabs
Kill the still-closing waters, as diminish
One dowle that's in my plume: my fellow-ministers
Are like invulnerable. If you could hurt,
Your swords are now too massy for your strengths,
And will not be uplifted...But, remember
(For that's my business to you!) that you three
From Milan did supplant good Prospero;   70
Exposed unto the sea—which hath requit it!—
Him, and his innocent child: for which foul deed
The powers, delaying, not forgetting, have
Incensed the seas and shores—yea, all the creatures,
Against your peace...Thee of thy son, Alonso,
They have bereft; and do pronounce by me,
Ling'ring perdition (worse than any death
Can be at once!) shall step by step attend
You, and your ways; whose wraths to guard you from—
Which here, in this most desolate isle, else falls   80
Upon your heads—is nothing but heart's sorrow,
And a clear life ensuing.

'*He vanishes in thunder: then, to soft music, enter the
shapes again, and dance, with mocks and mows, and
carrying out the table.*'

(*Prospero.* Bravely the figure of this harpy hast thou
Performed, my Ariel,—a grace it had, devouring:
Of my instruction hast thou nothing bated
In what thou hadst to say: so, with good life
And observation strange, my meaner ministers
Their several kinds have done: my high charms work,
And these, mine enemies, are all knit up
In their distractions: they now are in my power;   90

And in these fits I leave them, whilst I visit
Young Ferdinand—whom they suppose is drowned—
†And mine and his loved darling.   [*he departs*

admired / Miranda .

Gonzalo. I'th' name of something holy, sir, why
          stand you
In this strange stare?
     Alonso.   O, it is monstrous, monstrous!
Methought the billows spoke, and told me of it,
The winds did sing it to me; and the thunder,
That deep and dreadful organ-pipe, pronounced
The name of Prosper: it did bass my trespass.
100 Therefore my son i'th'ooze is bedded; and
I'll seek him deeper than e'er plummet sounded,
And with him there lie mudded. [*he rushes towards the sea*
     Sebastian.   But one fiend at a time,
I'll fight their legions o'er.
     Antonio.   I'll be thy second.
               [*they move away, distraught, sword in hand*

Guilt Complex

Gonzalo. All three of them are desperate: their
          great guilt,
Like poison given to work a great time after,
Now 'gins to bite the spirit: I do beseech you,
That are of suppler joints, follow them swiftly,
And hinder them from what this ecstasy
May now provoke them to.
     Adrian.   Follow, I pray you.
                         [*they pursue the madmen*

[4. 1.] *Before Prospero's cell.* PROSPERO *comes from the*
               cave with FERDINAND *and* MIRANDA.

Prospero. If I have too austerely punished you,
Your compensation makes amends, for I
Have given you here a third of mine own life,
Or that for which I live: who once again

*books
or Caliban or
Ariel after
parts*

I tender to thy hand...All thy vexations
Were but my trials of thy love, and thou
Hast strangely stood the test: here, afore Heaven,
I ratify this my rich gift: O Ferdinand,
†Do not smile at me that I boast hereof,
For thou shalt find she will outstrip all praise   10
And make it halt behind her.

   Ferdinand.   I do believe it
Against an oracle.

   Prospero. Then, as my gift, and thine own acquisition
Worthily purchased, take my daughter: but
If thou dost break her virgin-knot before
All sanctimonious ceremonies may
With full and holy rite be minist'red,
No sweet aspersion shall the heavens let fall
To make this contract grow; but barren hate,
Sour-eyed disdain and discord shall bestrew   20
The union of your bed with weeds so loathly
That you shall hate it both: therefore take heed,
As Hymen's lamp shall light you.

   Ferdinand.   As I hope
For quiet days, fair issue, and long life,
With such love as 'tis now, the murkiest den,
The most oppórtune place, the strong'st suggestion
Our worser genius can, shall never melt
Mine honour into lust, to take away
The edge of that day's celebration,
When I shall think, or Phœbus' steeds are foundered,   30
Or Night kept chained below.

   Prospero.   Fairly spoke;
Sit then, and talk with her, she is thine own...

   *The lovers draw apart and sit together on the bench of
           rock. Prospero lifts his staff.*
What, Ariel; my industrious servant Ariel!

ARIEL appears.

Ariel. What would my potent master? here I am.

Prospero. Thou and thy meaner fellows your last service
Did worthily perform: and I must use you
In such another trick: go, bring the rabble,
(O'er whom I give thee power) here, to this place:
Incite them to quick motion, for I must
40 Bestow upon the eyes of this young couple
Some vanity of mine art: it is my promise,
And they expect it from me.

Ariel.   Presently?

Prospero. Ay: with a twink.

Ariel. Before you can say 'come' and 'go,'
And breathe twice; and cry 'so, so',
Each one, tripping on his toe,
Will be here with mop and mow....
Do you love me, master? no?

Prospero. Dearly, my delicate Ariel...Do not approach,
50 Till thou dost hear me call.

Ariel.   Well: I conceive. [*vanishes*

Prospero [*turning to Ferdinand*]. Look thou be true: do
        not give dalliance
Too much the rein: the strongest oaths are straw
To th' fire i'th' blood: be more abstemious,
Or else good night your vow.

Ferdinand.   I warrant you, sir,
The white cold virgin snow upon my heart
Abates the ardour of my liver.

Prospero.   Well....
Now come my Ariel. Bring a corollary,
Rather than want a spirit; appear, and pertly!
No tongue...all eyes...be silent.   [*'soft music'*

a) gimmicky
b) laughes at Eliz. Theatre - very formal
c) Syne. of James I daughters marriage + Shakespeares. daughters marriage.
d) Break in play
e) Show of Prospero magic

THE MASQUE

IRIS appears.

Iris. Ceres, most bounteous lady, thy rich leas   60
Of wheat, rye, barley, vetches, oats, and pease;
Thy turfy mountains, where live nibbling sheep,
And flat meads thatched with stover, them to keep:
Thy banks with pionéd and twilléd brims,
Which spongy April at thy hest betrims—
To make cold nymphs chaste crowns; and thy
      broom-groves,
Whose shadow the dismisséd bachelor loves,
Being lass-lorn; thy poll-clipt vinéyard;
And thy sea-marge, sterile and rocky-hard,
Where thou thyself dost air—the queen o'th' sky,   70
Whose watry arch and messenger am I,
Bids thee leave these, and with her sovereign grace,
Here on this grass-plot, in this very place,
To come and sport: her peacocks fly amain:
                [*Juno's car appears in the sky*
Approach, rich Ceres, her to entertain.

Enter CERES.

Ceres. Hail, many-coloured messenger, that ne'er
Dost disobey the wife of Jupiter:
Who, with thy saffron wings, upon my flowers
Diffusest honey-drops, refreshing showers,
And with each end of thy blue bow dost crown   80
My bosky acres, and my unshrubbed down,
Rich scarf to my proud earth...why hath thy queen
Summoned me hither, to this short-grassed green?
    Iris. A contract of true love to celebrate,
And some donation freely to estate
On the blessed lovers.
      Ceres.   Tell me, heavenly bow,

If Venus or her son, as thou dost know,
Do now attend the queen? since they did plot
The means that dusky Dis my daughter got,
90 Her and her blind boy's scandalled company
I have forsworn.

    Iris.   Of her society
Be not afraid: I met her deity
Cutting the clouds towards Paphos; and her son
Dove-drawn with her: here thought they to have done
Some wanton charm upon this man and maid,
Whose vows are, that no bed-rite shall be paid
Till Hymen's torch be lighted: but in vain
Mars's hot minion is returned again
Her waspish-headed son has broke his arrows,
100 Swears he will shoot no more, but play with sparrows
And be a boy right out.

Juno alights from her car.

    Ceres.   Highest queen of state,
Great Juno comes; I know her by her gait.
    Juno. How does my bounteous sister? Go with me
To bless this twain, that they may prosperous be,
And honoured in their issue.   [*'they sing'*

    Juno.   Honour, riches, marriage-blessing,
           Long continuance, and increasing,
           Hourly joys be still upon you!
           Juno sings her blessings on you.
110 *Ceres.* Earth's increase, foison plenty,
           Barns and garners never empty,
           Vines with clustring bunches growing,
           Plants with goodly burden bowing;
           Spring come to you, at the farthest,
           In the very end of harvest!
           Scarcity and want shall shun you;
           Ceres' blessing so is on you.

Ferdinand. This is a most majestic vision, and
Harmonious charmingly: may I be bold
To think these spirits?
  Prospero.   Spirits, which by mine art   120
I have from their confines called to enact
My present fancies.
  Ferdinand.   Let me live here ever—
So rare a wond'red father and a wise
Makes this place Paradise.

    '*JUNO and CERES whisper, and send IRIS on employment*'
  Prospero.   Sweet, now silence:
Juno and Ceres whisper seriously.
  There's something else to do: hush, and be mute.
Or else our spell is marred.

  Iris. You nymphs, called Naiads, of the wand'ring
brooks,
With your sedged crowns and ever harmless looks,
Leave your crisp channels, and on this green land   130
Answer your summons; Juno does command....
Come, temperate nymphs, and help to celebrate
A contract of true love: be not too late.

            '*Enter certain Nymphs.*'
You sunburnt sicklemen, of August weary,
Come hither from the furrow, and be merry.
Make holiday: your rye-straw hats put on,
And these fresh nymphs encounter every one
In country footing.

'*Enter certain Reapers, properly habited: they join with the
Nymphs in a graceful dance; towards the end whereof
PROSPERO starts suddenly, and speaks; after which, to a
strange, hollow, and confused noise, they heavily vanish.*'

  Prospero [to himself]. I had forgot that foul conspiracy
Of the beast Caliban and his confederates   140

T.T.—7

Against my life: the minute of their plot
Is almost come: [*to the spirits*] Well done! avoid: no more.
  Ferdinand. This is strange: your father's in some passion,
That works him strongly.
  Miranda.   Never till this day,
Saw I him touched with anger so distempered.
  Prospero. You do look, my son, in a moved sort,
As if you were dismayed: be cheerful, sir.
Our revels now are ended...These our actors,
As I foretold you, were all spirits, and
150 Are melted into air, into thin air,
And, like the baseless fabric of this vision,
The cloud-capped towers, the gorgeous palaces,
The solemn temples, the great globe itself,
Yea, all which it inherit, shall dissolve,
And, like this insubstantial pageant faded,
Leave not a rack behind: we are such stuff
As dreams are made on; and our little life
Is rounded with a sleep...Sir, I am vexed.
Bear with my weakness, my old brain is troubled:
160 Be not disturbed with my infirmity.
If you be pleased, retire into my cell,
And there repose. A turn or two I'll walk,
To still my beating mind.
  Ferdinand, Miranda [*retiring*]. We wish your peace.
  Prospero. †Come with a thought; I think thee,
    Ariel: come.
                    ARIEL appears.
  Ariel. Thy thoughts I cleave to. What's thy pleasure?
  Prospero.   Spirit,
We must prepare to meet with Caliban.
  Ariel. Ay, my commander; when I presented Ceres,
I thought to have told thee of it, but I feared
Lest I might anger thee.

Prospero. Say again, where didst thou leave these varlets?   170
Ariel. I told you, sir, they were red-hot with drinking—
So full of valour, that they smote the air
For breathing in their faces: beat the ground
For kissing of their feet; yet always bending
Towards their project: Then I beat my tabor,
At which like unbacked colts they pricked their ears,
Advanced their eyelids, lifted up their noses,
As they smelt music. So I charmed their ears
That calf-like they my lowing followed, through
Toothed briers, sharp furzes, pricking gorse, and thorns,   180
Which ent'red their frail shins: at last I left them
I'th' filthy mantled pool beyond your cell,
There dancing up to th' chins, that the foul lake
†O'er-stunk their sweat.
Prospero.   This was well done, my bird.
Thy shape invisible retain thou still:
The trumpery in my house, go, bring it hither,
For stale to catch these thieves.
Ariel.   I go, I go.
Prospero. A devil, a born devil, on whose nature
Nurture can never stick: on whom my pains,
Humanely taken, all, all lost, quite lost—   190
And as with age his body uglier grows,
So his mind cankers. I will plague them all,
Even to roaring.

    ARIEL returns 'loaden with glistering apparel, etc.'
           Come, hang them on this line.

ARIEL hangs the garments on a tree. PROSPERO and ARIEL remain invisible. 'Enter CALIBAN, STEPHANO, and TRINCULO, all wet.'

Caliban. Pray you, tread softly, that the blind mole may
Not hear a foot fall: we now are near his cell.

Stephano. Monster, your fairy, which you say is a harm-less fairy, has done little better than played the Jack with us.

Trinculo. Monster, I do smell all horse-piss, at which my nose is in great indignation.

Stephano. So is mine. Do you hear, monster? If I should take a displeasure against you: look you. [*drawing a knife*

Trinculo. Thou wert but a lost monster.

Caliban [*grovelling*]. Good my lord, give me thy favour still.
Be patient, for the prize I'll bring thee to
Shall hoodwink this mischance: therefore, speak softly—
All's hushed as midnight yet. nnAure.   nature

Trinculo. Ay, but to lose our bottles in the pool,—

Stephano. There is not only disgrace and dishonour in that, monster, but an infinite loss.

Trinculo. That's more to me than my wetting: yet this is your harmless fairy, monster.

Stephano. I will fetch off my bottle, though I be o'er ears for my labour.

Caliban. Prithee, my king, be quiet,...[*crawling up to the cave*] Seest thou here,
This is the mouth o'th' cell...no noise, and enter...
Do that good mischief which may make this island
Thine own for ever, and I, thy Caliban,
For aye thy foot-licker.

Stephano. Give me thy hand. I do begin to have bloody thoughts.

Trinculo [*spies the apparel on the lime-tree*]. O King Stephano, O peer! [*seizes a gown*] O worthy Stephano, look what a wardrobe here is for thee!

Caliban. Let it alone, thou fool—it is but trash.

Trinculo. O, ho, monster: [*donning the gown*] we know what belongs to a frippery. O King Stephano! [*capers*

The 2 are very gullible +
Caliban becomes very angry

They
quarrel.

Stephano. Put off that gown, Trinculo. By this hand,
I'll have that gown.

Trinculo. Thy grace shall have it.　　[*he doffs it ruefully* 230

Caliban. The dropsy drown this fool! what do you mean,
†To dote thus on such luggage? Let't alone!
And do the murder first: if he awake,　*sickness of purpose.*
From toe to crown he'll fill our skins with pinches—
Make us strange stuff.

Stephano. Be you quiet, monster. Mistress line, is not
this my jerkin? [*putting it on*] Now is the jerkin under the
line: now jerkin you are like to lose your hair, and prove
a bald jerkin.

Trinculo. Do, do! We steal by line and level, an't like　240
your grace.

Stephano. I thank thee for that jest; here's a garment
for't: wit shall not go unrewarded while I am king of
this country: 'steal by line and level' is an excellent pass
of pate; there's another garment for't.

Trinculo. Monster, come, put some lime upon your
fingers, and away with the rest.

Caliban. I will have none on't: we shall lose our time,
And all be turned to barnacles, or to apes
With foreheads villainous low.　　　　　　　　　250

Stephano. Monster, lay-to your fingers: help to bear this
away where my hogshead of wine is, or I'll turn you out
of my kingdom: go to, carry this.

Trinculo. And this.

Stephano. Ay, and this.　　　　　　　　　[*they load him*

'*A noise of hunters heard. Enter divers spirits, in shape of
dogs and hounds, hunting them about; PROSPERO and
ARIEL setting them on.*'

Prospero. Hey, Mountain, hey!
Ariel. Silver...there it goes, Silver!

Prospero. Fury, Fury...there, Tyrant, there...hark, hark!
            [*Caliban, Stephano and Trinculo are driven out*

Go, charge my goblins, that they grind their joints
260 With dry convulsions, shorten up their sinews
With agéd cramps, and more pinch-spotted make them
Than pard or cat o' mountain.
    Ariel.   Hark, they roar.
    Prospero. Let them be hunted soundly...At this hour
Lies at my mercy all mine enemies:
Shortly shall all my labours end, and thou
Shalt have the air at freedom: for a little
Follow, and do me service.

[5. 1.] *They enter the cave and return, after a short pause;*
            PROSPERO '*in his magic robes.*'

    Prospero. Now does my project gather to a head:
My charms crack not: my spirits obey, and Time
Goes upright with his carriage...How's the day?
    Ariel. On the sixth hour, at which time, my lord,
You said our work should cease.
    Prospero.   I did say so,
When first I raised the tempest. Say, my spirit,
How fares the king and's followers?
    Ariel.   Confined together
In the same fashion as you gave in charge,
Just as you left them—all prisoners, sir,
10 In the line-grove which weather-fends your cell.
They cannot budge till your release: The king,
His brother, and yours, abide all three distracted;
And the remainder mourning over them,
Brimful of sorrow and dismay: but chiefly
Him you termed, sir, 'The good old lord, Gonzalo.'
His tears run down his beard, like winter's drops
From eaves of reeds...Your charm so strongly works 'em,

That if you now beheld them, your affections
Would become tender.

Prospero.   Dost thou think so, spirit?

Ariel. Mine would, sir, were I human.

Prospero.   And mine shall.... 20

Hast thou—which art but air—a touch, a feeling
Of their afflictions, and shall not myself,
One of their kind, that relish all as sharply,
Passion as they, be kindlier moved than thou art?
Though with their high wrongs I am struck to th' quick,
Yet, with my nobler reason, 'gainst my fury
Do I take part: the rarer action is
In virtue than in vengeance: they being penitent,
The sole drift of my purpose doth extend
Not a frown further. Go, release them, Ariel.   30
My charms I'll break, their senses I'll restore,
And they shall be themselves.

Ariel.   I'll fetch them, sir. [*vanishes*

Prospero [*traces a magic circle with his staff*]. Ye elves
    of hills, brooks, standing lakes and groves,
And ye, that on the sands with printless foot
Do chase the ebbing Neptune, and do fly him
When he comes back; you demi-puppets that
By moonshine do the green-sour ringlets make,
Whereof the ewe not bites: and you, whose pastime
Is to make midnight mushrooms, that rejoice
To hear the solemn curfew,—by whose aid,   40
†Weak ministers though ye be, I have bedimmed
The noontide sun, called forth the mutinous winds,
And 'twixt the green sea and the azured vault
Set roaring war: to the dread rattling thunder
Have I given fire, and rifted Jove's stout oak
With his own bolt: the strong-based promontory
Have I made shake, and by the spurs plucked up

The pine and cedar: graves at my command
Have waked their sleepers, oped, and let 'em forth
50 By my so potent art. But this rough magic
I here abjure: and, when I have required
Some heavenly music—which even now I do—

[*lifting his staff*

To work mine end upon their senses, that
This airy charm is for, I'll break my staff,
Bury it certain fathoms in the earth,
And deeper than did ever plummet sound
I'll drown my book.   ['*solemn music*'

'*Here enters* ARIEL *before: then* ALONSO, *with a frantic
gesture, attended by* GONZALO; SEBASTIAN *and* ANTONIO
in like manner, attended by ADRIAN *and* FRANCISCO:
they all enter the circle which PROSPERO *had made, and
there stand charmed; which* PROSPERO *observing, speaks.*'

A solemn air, and the best comforter   [*to Alonso*
To an unsettled fancy, cure thy brains,
60 Now useless boil within thy skull. There stand,
For you are spell-stopped....
Holy Gonzalo, honourable man,
Mine eyes, ev'n sociable to the show of thine,
Fall fellowly drops...The charm dissolves apace,
And as the morning steals upon the night,
Melting the darkness, so their rising senses
Begin to chase the ignorant fumes that mantle
Their clearer reason....O good Gonzalo,
My true preserver, and a loyal sir
70 To him thou follow'st; I will pay thy graces
Home, both in word and deed...Most cruelly
Didst thou, Alonso, use me and my daughter:
Thy brother was a furtherer in the act—
Thou art pinched for't now, Sebastian. Flesh and blood,

You, brother mine, that entertained ambition,
Expelled remorse and nature—who, with Sebastian,
(Whose inward pinches therefore are most strong)
Would here have killed your king—I do forgive thee,
Unnatural though thou art...Their understanding
Begins to swell, and the approaching tide
Will shortly fill the reasonable shores
That now lies foul and muddy. Not one of them
That yet looks on me, or would know me. Ariel,
Fetch me the hat and rapier in my cell.

> [*Ariel flits to the cave*

I will discase me, and myself present
As I was sometime Milan: quickly spirit,
Thou shalt ere long be free.

Returning '*ARIEL* sings, and helps to attire him.'

Ariel. Where the bee sucks, there suck I.
　　　　In a cowslip's bell I lie.
　　　　There I couch, when owls do cry.
　　　　On the bat's back I do fly
　　　　After summer merrily....
　Merrily, merrily, shall I live now,
　　Under the blossom that hangs on the bough.
　Prospero. Why, that's my dainty Ariel: I shall miss thee,
But yet thou shalt have freedom: so, so, so....

> [*as Ariel attires him*

To the king's ship, invisible as thou art—
There shalt thou find the mariners asleep
Under the hatches: the master and the boatswain
Being awake, enforce them to this place;
And presently, I prithee.
　Ariel. I drink the air before me, and return
Or ere your pulse twice beat.

> [*vanishes*

　Gonzalo. All torment, trouble, wonder, and amazement

They are
frightened

Inhabits here: some heavenly power guide us
Out of this fearful country.

Prospero.　　　　　　　Behold, sir king,
The wrongéd Duke of Milan, Prospero:
For more assurance that a living prince
Does now speak to thee, I embrace thy body,
And to thee and thy company I bid
A hearty welcome.

   Alonso.　　　　　Whe'er thou be'st he or no,
Or some enchanted trifle to abuse me,
As late I have been, I not know: thy pulse
Beats, as of flesh and blood: and, since I saw thee,
Th'affliction of my mind amends, with which
I fear a madness held me: this must crave—
An if this be at all—a most strange story.
Thy dukedom I resign, and do entreat
Thou pardon me my wrongs…But how should Prospero
Be living, and be here?

   Prospero [*to Gonzalo*].　First, noble friend,
Let me embrace thine age, whose honour cannot
Be measured or confined.

respect for
him.

   Gonzalo.　　　　　Whether this be
Or be not, I'll not swear.

   Prospero.　　　　　You do yet taste
Some subtilties o'th'isle, that will not let you
Believe things certain: Welcome, my friends all!
[*aside to Sebastian and Antonio*] But you, my brace of
  lords, were I so minded,
I here could pluck his highness' frown upon you,
And justify you traitors: at this time
I will tell no tales.

   Sebastian [*aside to Antonio*].　The devil speaks in him…

   Prospero.　No…
For you—most wicked sir—whom to call brother

Would even infect my mouth, I do forgive
Thy rankest fault—all of them; and require
My dukedom of thee, which, perforce, I know,
Thou must restore.

Alonso.   If thou beest Prospero,
Give us particulars of thy preservation,
How thou hast met us here, who three hours since *holding to time*
Were wrecked upon this shore; where I have lost—
How sharp the point of this remembrance is!—
My dear son Ferdinand.

Prospero.   I am woe for't, sir.   140
Alonso. Irreparable is the loss, and patience
Says it is past her cure.

Prospero.   I rather think
You have not sought her help, of whose soft grace
For the like loss I have her sovereign aid,
And rest myself content.

Alonso.   You the like loss?

Prospero. As great to me as late, and súpportable
To make the dear loss, have I means much weaker
Than you may call to comfort you; for I
Have lost my daughter.

Alonso.   A daughter?
O heavens, that they were living both in Naples,   150
The king and queen there! that they were, I wish
Myself were mudded in that oozy bed
Where my son lies...When did you lose your daughter?
Prospero. In this last tempest....I perceive these lords *dramatic irony*
At this encounter do so much admire
That they devour their reason, and scarce think
Their eyes do offices of truth, their words
Are natural breath: but, howsoe'er you have
Been justled from your senses, know for certain,
That I am Prospero, and that very duke   160

Which was thrust forth of Milan, who most strangely
Upon this shore, where you were wrecked, was landed,
To be the lord on't: No more yet of this,
For 'tis a chronicle of day by day,
Not a relation for a breakfast, nor
Befitting this first meeting: [*with his hand on the curtain
of the cave*] Welcome, sir;
This cell's my court: here have I few attendants,
And subjects none abroad: pray you, look in:
My dukedom since you have given me again,
170 I will requite you with as good a thing—
At least, bring forth a wonder, to content ye
As much as me my dukedom.

'*Here PROSPERO discovers FERDINAND and MIRANDA,
playing at chess.*'

Miranda. Sweet lord, you play me false.
Ferdinand.   †My dearest love,
I would not for the world.
Miranda. †Yet, for a score of kingdoms you should
wrangle,
And I would call it fair play.
Alonso.   If this prove
A vision of the island, one dear son
Shall I twice lose.
Sebastian.   A most high miracle!
Ferdinand. Though the seas threaten, they are merciful—
180 I have cursed them without cause.   [*he kneels*
Alonso [*embracing him*].   Now all the blessings
Of a glad father compass thee about:
Arise, and say how thou cam'st here.
Miranda.   O, wonder!
How many goodly creatures are there here!
How beauteous mankind is! O brave new world,

That has such people in't!

Prospero [smiling sadly].   'Tis new to thee.

Alonso. What is this maid, with whom thou wast at play?
Your eld'st acquaintance cannot be three hours:
Is she the goddess that hath severed us,
And brought us thus together?

Ferdinand.   Sir, she is mortal;
But, by immortal Providence, she's mine;   190
I chose her when I could not ask my father
For his advice, nor thought I had one: She
Is daughter to this famous Duke of Milan,
Of whom so often I have heard renown,
But never saw before: of whom I have
Received a second life; and second father
This lady makes him to me.

Alonso.   I am hers;
But O, how oddly will it sound, that I
Must ask my child forgiveness!

Prospero.   There, sir, stop.
Let us not burden our remembrance with   200
A heaviness that's gone.

Gonzalo.   I have inly wept,
Or should have spoke ere this...Look down, you gods,
And on this couple drop a blessèd crown;
For it is you that have chalked forth the way
Which brought us hither.

Alonso.   I say 'Amen,' Gonzalo.

Gonzalo. Was Milan thrust from Milan, that his issue
Should become kings of Naples? O, rejoice
Beyond a common joy, and set it down
With gold on lasting pillars: 'In one voyage
Did Claribel her husband find at Tunis,   210
And Ferdinand, her brother, found a wife,
Where he himself was lost, Prospero his dukedom

In a poor isle, and all of us ourselves,
When no man was his own.'

Alonso [*to Ferdinand and Miranda*]. Give me your hands:
Let grief and sorrow still embrace his heart
That doth not wish you joy.

Gonzalo.   Be it so, Amen.

'*Enter ARIEL with the MASTER and BOATSWAIN
amazedly following.*'

O look sir, look sir, here is more of us...
I prophesied, if a gallows were on land,
This fellow could not drown. [*to the Boatswain*] Now,
          blasphemy,
220 That swear'st grace o'er-board, not an oath on shore?
Hast thou no mouth by land?
What is the news?

Boatswain. The best news is, that we have safely found
Our king and company: the next, our ship,
Which, but three glasses since, we gave out split,
Is tight and yare and bravely rigged as when
We first put out to sea.

Ariel [*at Prospero's ear*]. Sir, all this service
Have I done since I went.

Prospero.   My tricksy spirit!

Alonso. These are not natural events—they strengthen
From strange to stranger: say, how came you hither?

230 *Boatswain.* If I did think, sir, I were well awake,
I'ld strive to tell you...We were dead of sleep,
And—how we know not—all clapped under hatches,
Where, but even now, with strange and several noises
Of roaring, shrieking, howling, jingling chains,
And moe diversity of sounds, all horrible,
We were awaked...straightway, at liberty;
Where we, in all her trim, freshly beheld

Our royal, good, and gallant ship: our master
Cap'ring to eye her…On a trice, so please you,
Even in a dream, were we divided from them,   240
And were brought moping hither.

    Ariel [*at Prospero's ear*].   Was't well done?

    Prospero. Bravely, my diligence,—thou shalt be free.

    Alonso. This is as strange a maze as e'er men trod,
And there is in this business more than nature
Was ever conduct of: some oracle
Must rectify our knowledge.

    Prospero.   Sir, my liege,
Do not infest your mind with beating on
The strangeness of this business. At picked leisure,
Which shall be shortly single, I'll resolve you—
Which to you shall seem probable—of every   250
These happened accidents: till when, be cheerful
And think of each thing well….[*to Ariel*] Come
      hither, spirit.
Set Caliban and his companions free:
Untie the spell…[*Ariel goes*] How fares my gracious sir?
There are yet missing of your company
Some few odd lads, that you remember not.

    '*Enter ARIEL, driving in CALIBAN, STEPHANO,
      and TRINCULO, in their stolen apparel.*'

    Stephano. Every man shift for all the rest, and let no
man take care for himself; for all is but fortune: coragio,
bully-monster, coragio!

    Trinculo. If these be true spies which I wear in my   260
head, here's a goodly sight.

    Caliban. O Setebos, these be brave spirits, indeed:
How fine my master is! I am afraid
He will chastise me.

    Sebastian.   Ha, ha!

What things are these, my lord Antonio?
Will money buy 'em?

Antonio.   Very like: one of them
Is a plain fish, and no doubt marketable.

Prospero. Mark but the badges of these men, my lords,

270 Then say if they be true. This mis-shaped knave— *hatred of*
His mother was a witch, and one so strong *anima, puts*
That could control the moon, make flows and ebbs, *him*
And deal in her command without her power.
These three have robbed me, and this demi-devil—
For he's a bastard one—had plotted with them
To take my life. Two of these fellows you
Must know and own, this thing of darkness I *prospero admits*
Acknowledge mine.

Caliban.   I shall be pinched to death.

Alonso. Is not this Stephano, my drunken butler?

Sebastian. He is drunk now; where had he wine?

280 *Alonso.* And Trinculo is reeling ripe: where should they
Find this grand liquor that hath gilded 'em?
How cam'st thou in this pickle?

Trinculo. I have been in such a pickle since I saw you
last that, I fear me, will never out of my bones: I shall
not fear fly-blowing.   [*Stephano groans*

Sebastian. Why, how now, Stephano?

Stephano. O, touch me not—I am not Stephano, but
a cramp.

Prospero. You'ld be king o'th'isle, sirrah?

290 *Stephano.* I should have been a sore one then.

Alonso. This is as strange a thing as e'er I looked on.
                   [*pointing at Caliban*

Prospero. He is as disproportioned in his manners
As in his shape. Go, sirrah, to my cell;
Take with you your companions; as you look
To have my pardon, trim it handsomely.

picking Prospero heart from fly-blowing.

using him in service — ie: forgiveness

Caliban. Ay, that I will: and I'll be wise hereafter,
And seek for grace. What a thrice-double ass
Was I, to take this drunkard for a god!
And worship this dull fool!

realizes how stupid he has been

Prospero.   Go to, away.

Alonso. Hence—and bestow your luggage where you
      found it.   300

Sebastian. Or stole it rather.

                    [*Caliban, Stephano and Trinculo slink off*

Prospero. Sir, I invite your Highness and your train
To my poor cell: where you shall take your rest
For this one night, which—part of it—I'll waste
With such discourse as, I not doubt, shall make it
Go quick away...the story of my life,
And the particular accidents gone by
Since I came to this isle: and in the morn
I'll bring you to your ship, and so to Naples,
Where I have hope to see the nuptial   310
Of these our dear-beloved solémnizéd—
And thence retire me to my Milan, where
Every third thought shall be my grave.

Shakespeare himself

Alonso.   I long
To hear the story of your life; which must
Take the ear strangely.

Prospero.   I'll deliver all—
And promise you calm seas, auspicious gales,
And sail so expeditious, that shall catch
Your royal fleet far off...My Ariel—chick,
That is thy charge: then to the elements
Be free, and fare thou well...[*bowing them in*] Please you
      draw near.   320

sets him free

  They all enter the cave: the curtain falls behind them.

EPILOGUE.

SPOKEN BY PROSPERO.

Now my charms are all o'erthrown,
And what strength I have's mine own,
Which is most faint: now, 'tis true,
I must be here confined by you,
Or sent to Naples. Let me not,
Since I have my dukedom got,
And pardoned the deceiver, dwell
In this bare island, by your spell.
But release me from my bands,
With the help of your good hands:
Gentle breath of yours my sails
Must fill, or else my project fails,
Which was to please: Now I want
Spirits to enforce...art to enchant—
And my ending is despair,
Unless I be reliev'd by prayer,
Which pierces so, that it assaults
Mercy itself, and frees all faults....
    As you from crimes would pardoned be,
Let your indulgence set me free.

THE COPY USED FOR
THE TEMPEST, 1623

There is no Quarto for *The Tempest*; and there seems good reason to suppose that the 'copy' for the Folio text was author's manuscript which had served as prompt-copy in the theatre. Prompt-copy in that age, however, might have a long history; and the condition of the Folio text appears to show that the *Tempest* MS had seen many changes before it reached the printer's hands. Something of the character of these changes may be gathered from a consideration of the following points:

(i) The traces of rhymed couplets at 3. 1. 24–5, 29–30; 3. 3. 32–3, 49–51, and elsewhere, together with the doggerel at 3. 2. 77–8 suggest that when Shakespeare took up *The Tempest* late in his career he had an old manuscript to go upon, possibly an early play of his own, which may have been related to the original of *Die Schöne Sidea*, a sixteenth century German drama with a kindred theme.

(ii) The received text has been clearly abridged, and abridged in the main by Shakespeare himself. The signs of this abridgment are many. *The Tempest* is the shortest text but one in the canon. Broken lines abound in it, as do passages of incorrect verse-lining—a sure sign of marginal alteration in a good text. The unsystematic mingling of verse and prose, e.g. in the wreck-scene and the Stephano scenes, point to the same conclusion, as also do characters like Antonio's son, who is referred to as being in the wreck but does not appear on the island, Francisco who appears, though seemingly by accident rather than design, and Trinculo who, though styled a 'jester' in the Folio 'names of the actors,' does very little to support this title, except to be called 'patch' and 'pied ninny' at one point. Perhaps however the clearest indication of all is the immense second scene, which comprises almost a quarter of the whole play. Most of this scene is taken up with an account of events which we may assume provided material for pre-wreck scenes in the earlier version. *The Tempest* is, indeed, remarkable in having three separate expositions: the story of Prospero and Miranda before they reached the island; the story of Sycorax, Caliban and Ariel; and in 2. 1. the story of Claribel and the African voyage. The threefold difficulty is tackled by Shakespeare with consummate skill; but the expositions are there, and they tell their own tale. At some stage of its evolution *The Tempest* was in all likelihood a loosely constructed drama, like *A Winter's Tale* and *Pericles*.

(iii) In one section of the play (i.e. 1. 2. 187–321), the abridgment is distinctly cruder and more drastic than elsewhere. The 'cuts' sometimes leave the sense obscure and tend to occur in the middle of speeches, while there are passages of verse which are both metrically and dramatically open to serious question.

(iv) The stage-directions of *The Tempest* possess a beauty and elaboration without parallel in the canon. They bear the unmistakable impress of the master's hand; but their presence suggests that the master himself did not contemplate personal supervision of the production for which they were written. Shakespeare retired to Stratford in 1611 and the abridgment may therefore have been carried through in his study at New Place.

(v) Lastly the Masque, which we can with certainty date early 1613 or Christmas 1612, appears to be an after-thought inserted into act 4 when the play had already taken final shape under Shakespeare's hand. Note: (1) 4. 1. 114–15,

> Spring come to you, at the farthest,
> In the very end of harvest!

'Spring' here is clearly a veiled reference to the 'off-spring' of the royal marriage (cf. 'issue' l. 105), since

nine months from the beginning of 1613 takes us to
'the very end of harvest.' (2) The Nymphs and
Reapers (cf. the dances, *Wint.* 4. 4.) seem originally
to have been intended to enter directly after Ariel's
words—

> Each one, tripping on his toe,
> Will be here with mop and mow.—

which announce the immediate advent of dancers; note
too Prospero's command 'incite them to quick motion'
l. 39. Ll. 48–138 are therefore presumably all additional
matter. (3) The introduction of the Masque strained the
resources of the King's men, as regards speaking parts;
Ariel has to play Ceres (ll. 167–9), which means a double
change of costume. (4) This in turn strained the dramatic structure of the scene, since Ariel must have time to
change. (5) He is allowed 25 lines in which to don his
Ceres dress; the interval being filled up partly by 'soft
music' and the Iris speech, partly by making Prospero
repeat the warning against pre-nuptial incontinency, already much better expressed in ll. 15–23. Note also that
the delay is inconsistent with Prospero's command 'Ay:
with a twink.' (6) Taking the entry of the Reapers
as the exit of Ceres, we have a dance and 22 lines before
Ariel returns in his own costume. Once again there is
undramatic delay, since it is absurd that Prospero should
pause to utter an irrelevant philosophical rhapsody when
he is evidently in great haste 'to prepare to meet with
Caliban.' However, even in the original, he had to dis-
miss the lovers; and it is noticeable that ll. 158–60 are
a direct rejoinder to Ferdinand's words at 143–4, and
that 'Sir, I am vexed' *completes* the line 'That works
him strongly*.'

* On the foregoing topic readers may be referred to
F. G. Fleay, *Life of Shakespeare*, pp. 249–50 and W. J.
Lawrence, *The Masque in The Tempest* (Fortnightly
Review, June 1920), the latter reaching our hands when
this volume was already in type.

Since the main purpose of the notes accompanying the present edition is to bring new textual facts to light rather than to formulate theories, there will be no attempt here to frame a hypothetical history of the *Tempest* MS in order to explain the phenomena noted above. Uncertainty as to the genuineness of an important piece of external evidence would in any event render such an attempt hazardous; for, while we know that *The Tempest* was performed at Court during the winter of 1612–13 in connexion with the festivities preceding the marriage of the Princess Elizabeth to the Elector Palatine, the entry in the Revels Accounts recording an earlier Court performance on Nov. 1, 1611 is still tainted with suspicions of forgery, though its authenticity has recently been defended with great force (v. pp. xlv, 109). One point, however, may legitimately be insisted upon. The crudity of the abridgment in the second section of act I scene 2 is the most striking bibliographical feature of the *Tempest* text; and students may well ask themselves (*a*) whether it is not connected with the introduction of the Masque, which would naturally involve curtailment somewhere else; and if so (*b*) whether Shakespeare can be held responsible for it. It should be noted in this connexion that the famous epilogue to the Masque, beginning 'Our revels now are ended' (4. 1. 148–58), though dramatically inappropriate in the text as it stands and clumsily linked up with what precedes (v. note 4. 1. 146), is undoubtedly by Shakespeare, and Shakespeare at his very best.

Such are the chief problems of the *Tempest* text. It will be convenient, in conclusion, to bring together, in the form of a scene by scene examination of the original edition, the bibliographical evidence for the abridgment and revision referred to in §§ ii and iii above.

Act one, scene one. Probably a verse-scene in the original unrevised play. Ll. 59–65 arranged as verse in F.;

and seven other verse-lines have been recovered, partly by expanding contractions.

Act one, scene two. This long scene falls dramatically into four clearly marked sections; and it is very significant that bibliographical disturbance is almost entirely confined to one of them. In § *a* (Dialogue between Prospero and Miranda, ll. 1–186) there is a single broken line, i.e. 159; in § *c* (the Caliban episode, ll. 322–75) we have broken lines at 325, 349, 350, and incorrectly divided verse at 362–3; in §*d* (the Ferdinand episode, ll. 375–506) there are no bibliographical peculiarities at all. But matters are very different in §*b* (Dialogue between Prospero and Ariel, ll. 187–305, followed by a short link passage, ll. 306–21). First there are five broken lines: 188, 195, 253, 317, 321, one of which, viz. 253, points to a glaring 'cut.' Next we have incorrect verse-lining at 310, together with two instances of obscurity in meaning (v. notes at ll. 261, 266) which can be readily explained by 'cuts' in the text. Lastly there are two further passages which must be considered in detail:

281–6. *Then was this island...I keep in service.* Note (1) This passage is a violent digression. (2) Omit it, and the context flows straight on. (3) The F. has a comma after 'in service,' which is absurd. (4) Ariel, who cleaves to Prospero's very thoughts (4. 1. 165), is extraordinarily obtuse here. Is it possible to avoid the conclusion that these five lines are an addition, a piece of patchwork, designed to compensate for a rent elsewhere in this section? The reason for their introduction is not far to seek; Caliban is to enter at l. 321, and this is the first mention of his name!

298–305. *Do so...diligence.* Correct lining and scansion are impossible. Ll. 301–5, taken with Ariel's momentary 'fine apparition' at l. 318 (in order, it seems, to exhibit his nymph's costume to the audience), is crudely theatrical, while the words 'Be subject to no sight but thine and mine: invisible to every eye-ball else' are surely absurd. The whole thing, in short, is suggestive of botchery; the F. repetition of *Pro.* at the beginning of l. 306 indicating a 'join' in the MS.

Act two, scene one. The chief bibliographical feature of this scene is the mingling of prose and verse, which divides it into five sections: (*a*) 1–9, all verse; (*b*) 10–104, all prose or prose-lined; (*c*) 105–138, all verse; (*d*) 139–187, verse mixed with prose; and (*e*) 188–324, all verse. Such regularity cannot be accidental; and is independent of the characters speaking, since Gonzalo talks both prose and verse, while Antonio and Sebastian talk prose in § *b*, verse in § *e*, and in § *d* now one and now the other. The prose or part-prose sections probably represent pages of the MS which have undergone revision.

Act two, scene two. F. prints ll. 1–17 as verse, and the rest (except for the songs, and three isolated lines) as prose, although most of Caliban's lines are really verse. This points to revision of the MS, from l. 18 onwards. The prose speeches, moreover, are very irregularly divided, as if they had been cut about in the MS.

Act three, scene one. No marks of revision.

Act three, scene two. Verse mingled with prose. Caliban generally, but not always, speaks verse (some of which is printed as prose), and in conversation with him Stephano occasionally breaks into verse also. Probably the whole scene was originally in verse.

Act three, scene three. Marks of revision, slight; but note broken lines 19, 52, 82, 93.

Act four, scene one. See § v above. Little bibliographical disturbance; no irregular lining, while the ten broken lines (59, 105, 127, 138, 169, 207, 219, 235, 250, 267) can mostly be explained by the exigencies of the Masque-verse and the mingling of verse and prose in the second half of the scene.

Act five, scene one. Broken lines at 57, 61, 87, 101, 103, 172, 174, 264, 282, 301, some of which may have arisen from revision. The extra-metrical and detached

'No' given to Prospero at l. 130 is curious and can best be explained by a 'cut' in the text which deprived us of the rest of the retort. Further the extreme awkwardness of l. 250, 'Which to you...of every,' suggests adaptation. Finally an important point is to be noted, viz. that this is the only occasion, apparently, in the whole canon where speakers who have concluded one scene appear again at the opening of the next. It is practically certain that some intervening scene has been deleted between 4. 1. and 5. 1.

D. W.

TRANSCRIPT OF THE FACSIMILE FROM *SIR THOMAS MORE*

all	marry god forbid that	1

moo   nay certainly yo^u ar
for to the king god hath his offyc lent
of dread of Iustyce, power and Comaund
hath bid him rule, and willd yo^u to obay   5
and to add ampler matie to this
he [god] hath not [le] souly lent the king his figure
his throne [hys] & sword, but gyven him his owne name
calls him a god on earth, what do yo^u then
rysing gainst him that god himsealf enstalls   10
but ryse gainst god, what do yo^u to yor sowles
in doing this o desperat [ar] as you are.
wash your foule mynds w^t teares and those same hande
that yo^u lyke rebells lyft against the peace
lift vp for peace, and your vnreuerent knees   15
[that] make them your feet to kneele to be forgyven

Notes. Sir Thomas More, haranguing a crowd of London
apprentices on 'ill May-day' 1517, reminds them that in
rising against the king's authority they are in rebellion
against God Himself.
    Deleted words or letters are printed in brackets.
    1. The rule indicates the beginning of a new speech.
2. 'moo'=a contraction for 'Moore,' i.e. Sir Thomas
More. 7. =solely.

NOTES

All significant departures from the Folio, including important emendations in punctuation, are recorded; the name of the critic who first suggested a reading being placed in brackets. Illustrative spellings and misprints are quoted from the Good Quarto texts (v. T.I. p. xxx), or from the F. when no Good Quarto exists. The line-numeration for references to plays not yet issued in this edition is that used in Bartlett's *Concordance*.

F., unless otherwise specified, stands for the First Folio; T.I. = Textual Introduction; Facs. = the facsimile, given herewith, of a passage from the 'Shakespearian' Addition to *Sir Thomas More*; Dryden = Dryden and D'Avenant's version of *The Tempest*; N.E.D. = *The New English Dictionary*; Sh. Eng. = *Shakespeare's England*; S.D. = stage-direction; G. = Glossary.

Characters in the Play. A reprint, in modern spelling, of the 'Names of the actors' at the end of the F. text. The F. spells Antonio throughout as 'Anthonio'; and Gonzalo sometimes (e.g. 2. 1. 262; 3. 3. 1 S.D.; 5. 1. 15, 62, 68) as 'Gonzallo.'

Acts and Scenes. Regularly divided throughout in F.; but v. p. 85.

I. I.

An excellent technical account of the seamanship in this scene is given in Sh. Eng. i. pp. 161–2.

1. *Bos'n* F. prints 'Bote-ſwaine' fourteen times, and 'Boſon' once (l. 12) by inadvertence. On principles of T.I. p. xl, 'Boſon' is the Shakespearian spelling. 'Boatswain' is retained at l. 9, as befitting the speech of a king.

10. *Play the men* v. G.

16. *care* (Rowe) F. 'cares'; compositor's grammar. *roarers*, with a play upon 'roaring boy,' a roistering bully.

20. *Councillor* F. 'Counsellor'; but 'Councellor' in
'Names of the actors.' Both meanings spelt 'Counsaylor'
by Shakespeare. Gonzalo was a member of the King's
Council, whose business it was to quell riots and 'work
the peace.' Cf. 'roarers' (l. 16), *M.W.W.* I. I. 35 and
Sh. Eng. ii. 384–5.

50. *two courses. Off* F. 'two courſes off'

50–1. *fireballs* (S.D.), i.e. St Elmo's fire. Cf. I. 2.
196–206.

52. *pulling out a bottle* (S.D.), cf. 'mouths be cold,'
'drunkards' and 'wide-chopped rascal' in text.

57–8. *lie drowning* etc., v. G.

65. *long heath, brown firs* Most edd. read 'brown
furze,' unnecessarily. F. spells 'firs' as 'firrs'; and at
4. I. 180 'furzes' as 'firzes.' The 'long heath' is the
'barren ground,' not heather.

I. 2.

4. *to th' welkin's cheek* v. G. 'cheek.'

7. The bracket (F.) is a revelation here. Miranda is
fey, and the spell of the 'noble creature' (Ferdinand) is
already upon her. v. Introd. p. li.

29. *soil* (Johnson) F. 'ſoule,' which most edd. read.
Note (1) 'soul' introduces a violent anacoluthon, de-
manding a colon at least; there is no stop of any kind at
the end of the line in F.; (2) the unsoiled garments of
the castaways is a recurring motive of the play; a lengthy
dialogue turns on it at 2. I. 61–105, while I. 2. 217

...Not a hair perished:
On their sustaining garments not a blemish,

is almost a repetition of the present passage; (3) the
difference between 'ſoile' and 'ſoule' is one minim-
stroke only; v. the *i* in 'forbid,' l. 1, Facs.

59. *A princess* (Pope) F. 'And Princeſſe'; compositor
hypnotised by 'and thy father,' 'and his only,' which
precede.

100. *Who having into truth* etc. Much annotated,

and clearly corrupt. Read *minted* for 'into,' and the whole context gains; 'telling' (i.e. counting it over), 'credit his own lie,' 'out o'th' substitution' (i.e. of the baser metal), and 'executing th'outward face of royalty, with all prerogative' (i.e. stamping the coin)—all carry on the idea of 'minting.' Further, the N.E.D. quotes Henry More (1664), 'Though it were in our power to mint Truth as we please...yet should we find it would not serve all emergencies,' where the parallel is exact. The misprint may be explained thus:—Shakespeare wrote 'minted' with one or two minims short, and with the *ed* like *oe*; this the compositor read as 'inntoe' or 'intoe' and set up as 'into.' v. T.I. pp. xli–xlii. Possibly, also 'sinner' (F. 'fynner,' though always apparently spelt 'finner' elsewhere in F.) is a misprint for 'fyner' or 'finer,' an official at the Mint, v. N.E.D.

109. *me* F. 'Me,' the capital denoting emphasis.

114. *Subject his 'coronet' to his 'crown'* F. 'Subiect his Coronet, to his Crowne,' where the emphasis-capitals and the comma-pause bring out the sarcasm in Prospero's voice.

137. *upon us* F. 'vpon's'

140. *Dear, they durst not,/So dear the love* etc. This play is noticeably full of such verbal echoes (cf. 'th' purpose,' ll. 129, 131, 'wicked,' ll. 321, 322, 'deservedly... deserved,' ll. 362, 363, and 'merchant,' 2. 1. 5), signs possibly of hasty revision on Shakespeare's part.

145–6. *they prepared/A rotten carcass of a butt* Much annotated, some supposing that 'butt' means 'botto,'² a kind of galliot. But Prospero is only speaking contemptuously of 'a rotten old tub,' as we should say.

155. *decked* Generally explained as 'sprinkled,' but N.E.D. gives no support. Read *eked*, i.e. increased (v. N.E.D. and *M.V.* 3. 2. 23); Prospero's tears added salt to salt. Shakespeare probably wrote 'eekt' with an oversized initial and the compositor took it for 'dekt.' v. T.I. p. xli and cf. *e* and *d* of 'rule' and 'bid,' Facs. l. 5.

159. *By Providence divine....* F. 'By prouidence di-uine,'. The isolated half-line and the comma suggest a 'cut' here. Prospero never answers Miranda's question.

173. *princes* (Rowe) F. 'Princeſſe' Shakespeare would spell 'princess' as 'princes,' avoiding as was his habit final *ss* or *sse*, but here the compositor has taken 'princes' for 'princess'—wrongly.

175. *Heaven* F. 'Heuen' (some copies): other copies read 'Heuens'

195. *To every article....* Broken line, suggesting 'cut'; we are entering the second section of the scene. v. p. 83.

201. *lightnings* (Theobald) F. 'lightning'; com-positor's grammar.

209. *fever of the mad* Dryden, followed by Rowe, prints 'mind'; which gives a better reading. In Shake-speare's hand, *min* might easily be read *ma*. v. Facs. for open *a* in 'all' l. 1, and 'enstalls' l. 10, and cf. T.I. p. xli.

211–12. *quit the vessel; then all afire* By restoring the F. punctuation we get a fine glimpse of Ferdinand hunted overboard by Ariel. All mod. edd. take 'then all afire with me' as referring to the ship.

240. *At least two glasses* v. G. 'glass.'

248. *made no mistakings* (Ritson) F. 'made thee no mistakings'; compositor hypnotised by 'prithee,' 'done thee,' 'told thee.'

249. *didst* F. 'did'

253. *Of the salt deep,* F. 'Of the ſalt deepe;' Strong-ly suggestive of a 'cut'; the F. semi-colon increasing the probability.

261. *O, was she so.* Prospero is about to contradict Ariel but does not do so; and the text leaves us in doubt as to the birthplace of Sycorax. The best explanation is a 'cut,' possibly in the middle of l. 263.

266. *one thing* Another obscurity, to be explained by another 'cut.' Note, too, the extra-metrical 'Ay, sir' l. 268; it looks as if 'Is not this true? *Ariel.* Ay, sir.' is a piece of patchwork to cover up the 'cut.' Charles

Lamb (v. Variorum *Tempest*) suggests that Shakespeare was thinking of the story of the witch who saved Algiers from Charles V in 1541 by raising a storm which dispersed his fleet.

269. *blew-eyed hag* Mod. edd. read 'blue' for F. 'blew,' which was a common 16th cent. spelling. Staunton, followed by G. C. Macaulay (*Mod. Lang. Rev.* xi. 75), suggests 'blear' (spelling 'bler'). The difference between *r* and *w* might be very slight in an 'English' hand; cf. '*r*ule' and '*w*illd' l. 5, Facs.

271. *wast* (Rowe) F. 'was'

281–6. *Then was this island...I keep in service* v. p. 83.

282. *she*. F. 'he.'

298–305. v. p. 83. F. divides ll. 301–2 'Go make... o'th' Sea,/Be subiect...inuisible'

306. *Awake* etc. F. repeats the indicator *Pro.* at the beginning of this line, v. p. 84.

310–11. *'Tis a villain...look on.* One line in F.

333. *camest* F. 'cam'st'

334. F. reading retained for sake of euphony. Most edd. read 'Thou strok'dst me and mad'st much of me,' which is horrible. Shakespeare probably wrote 'strokes' and 'mades,' *es* for *est* being a frequent form with him. He wrote to be heard, not to be read.

340. *Cursèd* (Steevens) F. 'Curs'd'

343. *sty me* F. 'Sty-me,' the hyphen indicative of the force of bitterness which Caliban throws on to the first word. v. Simpson, *Shakespearian Punctuation*, pp. 86–7.

352. *Miranda*. So F., but most edd. have preferred to give this speech to Prospero. Yet Caliban refers to her tuition at 2. 2. 145, while 1. 2. 120 shows that she was not ignorant of life.

357. *meaning*, F. 'meaning;'

359. *vile* F. 'vild'

362–63. F. divides: 'this Rocke, who hadst/Derseru'd more.' The rough verse, the broken line and the echo 'deservedly...deserved' all suggest hasty revision.

367. *be quick thou'rt best* Absence of punctuation denotes rapid delivery.

371. *achës* Pronounced 'aitches.'

378. *kissed*— No stop in F. Three motions before the dance: take hands, curtsey; kiss.

381–82. *bear/The burthen* We follow F. (most edd. read 'the burthen bear'), and arrange the song accordingly.

414. *What is't? a spirit?* F. 'What is't a Spirit?,' which leaves the pointing ambiguous.

420. *touching her cheek* (S.D.) supported by the significant F. brackets enclosing 'that's beauty's canker.' The faces of both lovers are tear-stained 'at their first meeting; Shakespeare does not do these things by accident.

442–43. *the Duke of Milan/And his brave son* The sole mention of Antonio's son in the text. He must have been one of the Alonso group in the earlier version (v. note 2. 1. 112). Prospero's effective retort made a 'cut' difficult.

455. *in either's power* (Rowe) F. 'in eythers powers'

464–65. F. prefixes *Pro.* to both lines, cf. 1. 306 and p. 84. But repetition here occurs at the turn of a page, and may be due to compositor, though he gives *Pro.* as the catch-word.

489. *again,* F. 'againe.'

2. 1.

11. *The visitor* etc. v. G. 'visitor.' The words anticipate Sebastian's at ll. 191–93 which are probably additional matter, v. note ll. 189–99.

16–17. F. arranges thus: 'When euery greefe is entertaind,/That's offer'd comes to th'entertainer.'

29. *The old cock.* Note other references to Gonzalo's bird-like appearance in this scene, e.g. 'fowl weather' l. 141, 'bat-fowling' l. 182 (v. G.), 'chough' l. 263. Possibly jests upon the head-gear of the old Councillor, cf. note l. 65.

32. *laughter* a sitting of eggs, v. N.E.D., cf. 'cock,' 'cockerel,' 'begins to crow,' in text.

36. *So! you're paid.* F. 'So: you'r paid.' F. gives the laugh to Sebastian and the comment to Antonio, transposing the names. Antonio wins the bet, and his 'laughter' (v. previous note) is his payment.

55. *eye* spot. Sebastian seems to refer to Gonzalo, who was perhaps dressed in green. He was a small man; v. 'morsel' l. 283.

62–3. *freshness and gloss, as being* F. 'freſhneſſe and gloſſes, being.' The emendation seems self-evident.

65. *pockets* Puzzling; but Gonzalo, being like a cock (v. l. 29), had perhaps the cock's red wattles or 'wallets' (cf. 3. 3. 46).

77. *Widow Dido!* Perhaps Antonio pronounces it 'widdow Diddo.' Probably some topical allusion, perhaps to Chapman's *Widow's Tears* (c. 1605) performed at Court Feb. 20, 1613. Cf. 'Temperance' G.

90. *pocket*, cf. l. 65. The 'pocket' was evidently a large one.

93. F. reads '*Gon*. I.', and some edd. '*Gon*. Ay.' which is obvious though pointless, while others interpret it as a sigh from Alonso. Perhaps the most satisfactory reading would be '*Gonzalo [rousing the king]*. Sir!' Antonio's comment, 'Why, in good time,' harking back to 'One...tell' l. 15, gives us the clue. Gonzalo, after a long pause, once again attempts to act 'visitor,' and Antonio means that 'the watch of his wit' is striking two. The misprint can be explained by supposing that 'sir' was written close to 'gon' in the MS, and that the compositor took 'gonsir!' as 'gonsa I.' In careless 'English' script *ir* could be confused with *a*, v. *Lear*, 1. 1. 39, 'first' misprinted for 'fast.'

112. F. gives the speech to Francisco, and the MS must be responsible. Yet the lines, as the play stands, would seem to belong to Gonzalo, since they alone give point to Antonio's gibe, ll. 228–35. Francisco's name

occurs in the F. entries at 2. 1. 1 S.D.; 3. 3. 1 S.D.; and
5. 1. 57 S.D.; but, beyond this speech, he has only three
words to say in the whole drama, i.e. 3. 3. 40. He is,
therefore, probably a relic of the earlier version like
Antonio's son, cf. 1. 2. 442 and p. 79. N.B. a Prince
Franciscus is one of two Councillors attending the
usurping Duke in *Die Schöne Sidea*. v. pp. xlix, 79.

119. *th' shore*... F. 'th' shore;'

124. *loose* So F. All edd. read 'lose'; but 'loose her
to an African' (i.e. turn her loose to a black-man) is
more forcible and appropriate to the speaker. Cf. *M.W.W.*
2. 1. 190, and *Ham.* 2. 2. 162.

130. *sh'ould* (i.e. she should) F. 'fhould' Malone
suggested 'she'd.'

135. broken line.

162. *it* Often used as genitive in 16th cent.

165–66. *None, man* etc. F. prints comma after 'knaves'
and colon after 'sir,' transposing original punctuation.

167–68. F. prints the 'and' with 'do you mark me,
sir?'; our emendation follows a suggestion of Aldis
Wright's. F. error suggests hasty revision.

185–86. *laugh me asleep* At this period 'laugh' was
commonly spelt and pronounced 'loffe,' cf. *M.N.D.*
2. 1. 55; 'loffe' was also a 16th cent. spelling of 'luff.'
Gonzalo is here perhaps punning on the two words, 'to
luff asleep' being a nautical term meaning 'to draw into
the wind, so that the ship stops,' v. N.E.D. Asleep, 5;
Luff. Note 'heavy' = going slow (naut.).

189–99. F. arranges: 'Would...thoughts,/I find...so./
Please you sir,/Do...it:/It seldom...comforter./We two
...person,/While you...safety.' Again at 198 it gives
'Doth it...I find/Not myself...sleep.' All this is strongly
suggestive of revision, the first passage, unrevised, reading apparently—

Would (with themfelves) fhut vp my thoughts.

We two my lord,

200. *consent;* F. 'confent'

218. *Trebles thee o'er.* F. 'Trebbles thee ore.' Read *troubles* for 'trebles' (an *e:o* misprint, v. T.I. p. xlii; possibly spelt 'trovbles,' the *v* being mistaken for *b*, v. 'vp' l. 15, Facs.). The next line—'standing water'— requires 'troubles,' cf. *Shrew* 5. 2. 142 'A woman moved is like a fountain troubled.' Antonio suggests that it bores Sebastian to 'heed' him; 'over-trouble' = to put to too much trouble (v. N.E.D.). Rowe (2nd. ed.) reads 'troubles'

232–33. *only professes* etc. Gonzalo is a Privy Councillor.

240. *But douts discovery there* (Nicholson). 'dout'=do out, extinguish. F. reads 'doubt' which most edd. follow. 'Doubts' is printed for 'douts' in F. *Ham.* 4. 7. 192; the trouble being that 'dout' was a common 16th cent. spelling for 'doubt.' Thus emended, the passage means: 'Even Ambition cannot look beyond a crown, but there puts out her torch of discovery.'

241–42. *Then, tell...Naples?* One line in F.

247. *she that...from whom* etc. F. 'she that from whom' The sense is clear but many suspect corruption; if so, it was probably due to the hypnotic influence of the three previous 'she that's which led the compositor to set the words up once again in place of something else, e.g. 'sailing,' cf. note 1. 2. 59.

296. *thee* (Dyce) F. 'them' 'The' was a Shakespearian spelling for 'thee,' and the compositor here, perhaps, took it for 'thē.'

304–6. F. arranges: '*Gon.* Now...king./*Alon.* Why how...drawn?/Wherefore...looking?/*Gon.* What's the matter?'—which is quite impossible in view of Alonso's statement that he 'heard nothing' l. 310, and of Gonzalo's speech, ll. 314–19. Our arrangement is based upon suggestions by Staunton and Dyce.

2. 2.

63. *as ever went on four legs.* The Caliban-Trinculo quadruped obliges Stephano to change the 'two legs' of the proverb to 'four legs.'

65. *at' nostrils,* i.e. at the nostrils. Some interpret as 'at 's nostrils.'

82. *by thy trembling.* The drunkard's hand shakes.

86. *cat.* Alluding to proverb 'good liquor will make a cat speak' (Steevens).

91. *O, defend me!* A space in the F. before 'O' suggests that the word 'God' has been omitted because of the blasphemy law.

120. *These...sprites.* **144.** *I have...adore thee.* **167.** *A plague...serve* F. preserves verse arrangement for these isolated lines.

163–64. *An abominable monster!* Exclamation perhaps caused by a glimpse of Caliban from behind, as he bends to kiss Stephano's foot.

177. *scamels* Many emendations, the chief candidates being: (1) 'staniels,' i.e. kestrels; but Shakespeare mentions staniels twice elsewhere (F. *Tw. Nt.* 2. 5. 124; Q2 *Ham.* 2. 2. 615) and uses the alternative form 'stallion' on both occasions; (2) 'seamells,' i.e. seamews, which are referred to in Strachey's *Letter* (1610), from which Shakespeare drew some local colour for *The Tempest.* 'Seamells,' therefore, holds the field. Palaeographically, there is nothing to choose between the two, since each has three minim-strokes in the middle of the word, and examples of *t:c* and *e:c* misprints both occur in the Qq.

188. *trenchering* Many edd. read 'trencher' for metrical reasons, forgetting that Caliban is drunk; cf. the extra-metrical 'Margery,' 2. 2. 50.

3. 1.

15. *Most busie lest, when I doe it.* This line, the prize crux of *The Tempest* text, is given exactly as the F. prints it. All critics agree as to the general sense, which is perhaps best expressed in Spedding's proposed reading: 'Most busiest when idlest.' The usual reading in mod. editions is 'Most busy, least when I do it,' against which there are two objections: it is generally felt to be awkward, and it involves the alteration of the comma, a serious point in this carefully punctuated text. We suggest that 'busie lest' is a misprint for *busy-idlest* (i.e. employed in trifles), which Shakespeare wrote in one word and spelt 'bizyydlest'; 'bizy' being quite a possible phonetic spelling, while 'ydle' is not infrequent in Shakespearian texts. If so, it is not difficult to see how the misprint arose. The letters *e* and *d*, and *z* and *y* being very similar in 'English' script, the compositor simply misdivided the word and read 'bizzye lest.' Cf. 'Busy idlenesse' Gabriel Harvey (Grosart i. 213). There remains 'do it,' which is conceivably a misprint for 'dote.' Not only is 'doote' a common form with Shakespeare for 'do it,' but we also get 'dooting' (*Troil.* 5. 4. 4) and 'dooters' (*L.L.L.* 4. 3. 260) for 'doting' and 'doters.'

24–5. Note internal rhyme, 'while...pile,' v. p. 79.

29–30. *do it...to it*; more rhymes, but terminal this time.

33–4. *'tis fresh morning* etc. This is curious, as the lovers had never been in each other's company at night. Possibly a relic of the earlier version.

3. 2.

4–5. *The folly of this island!* Pointless as it stands, despite the reference to weak brains. King Stephano asks Caliban to pledge him, but Caliban is beyond speech. The task, therefore, falls to Trinculo; who toasts his majesty, the words he utters being, we suggest, *the Sophy of this island!* 'Sophy,' which Shakespeare uses thrice elsewhere, was in his day the title of the Shah of Persia. But it also meant a wise man, and was used of the Magi; hence, by a natural train of thought, Trinculo's talk of 'brains.' Shakespeare used *ph* and *f* interchangeably;

and 'ſofy' might easily be read as 'foly,' cf. 'gift' for 'gilt,' *L.L.L.* 5. 2. 652.

42–4. *As I...island* F. arranges as prose.

56. *I will* F. 'Ile'

77–8. F. arrangement. A piece of clown-doggerel, such as Speed uses in *Two Gent.*; probably fossil from the earlier version. v. p. 79.

120. *cout'em* Mod. edd. read 'scout.'

125. *Nobody.* v. G.

129. *He that...debts* Proverbial; v. Apperson, *English Proverbs*, 'Death squares all accounts'

3. 3.

2. *ache* F. 'akes'; compositor's grammar.

13–14. *The next...throughly.* One line in F.

29. *islanders* (F2) F. 'Islands'

32–3. *kind...find.* Another internal rhyme. v. p. 79.

32. *gentle-kind* (Theobald) F. 'gentle, kind,' cf. note 4. 1. 106.

39. *Praise in departing.* v. G.

40. *Francisco.* v. note 2. 1. 112. Here again it might be better to give the speech to Gonzalo.

43. This speech may belong to Antonio. (*a*) 'When we were boys' would be appropriate to him, and not to the older Gonzalo. (*b*) The words continue the strain of mock-credulity in ll. 21–27. (*c*) It is surely part of the magic that the 'three men of sin' should find the banquet attractive, Alonso less so than the others because his sin was less. (*d*) If Gonzalo persuades the king to partake, why does he not partake himself? And if the words are Antonio's, then the reference to goitre, which has puzzled many, may be another hit at Gonzalo; cf. 'pockets,' note 2. 1. 65.

50–1. *last...past.* Another internal rhyme. v. p. 79.

55. *what is in't, the* F. 'what is in 't: the'

56. *to belch up—yea* (Staunton) F. 'to belch vp you;' 'Yea' is surely right, 'belch up you' being in-

tolerably awkward. The misprint was perhaps partly caused by the semi-colon after 'yea' in the MS, a natural pause but confusing if no comma followed 'up.' It is noteworthy that the punctuation is careless throughout this speech.

61. *fate. The* F. 'fate, the'

70. *Prospero*; F. 'Prospero,'

79. *ways*; F. 'wayes,'

84. *devouring* Possibly a minim-misprint for 'devoiring,' i.e. serving, waiting at table.

86–7. *with good life|And observation strange,* i.e. to the life (or 'with liveliness') and with rare compliance. For 'strange,' cf. 'strangely,' 4. 1. 7.

93. *And his and mine loved darling.* Edd. quote as parallels 'in yours and my discharge,' 2. 1. 251, and 'by hers and mine adultery,' *Cym.* 5. 5. 186. But here we have 'mine' before a consonant, not found, apparently, elsewhere in Shakespeare. The simplest emendation would be, of course, to read 'my'; but it is possible that 'and mine' is a misprint for 'admired,' *mird* being read as *mine*—a combined minim and *e:d* misprint. If so Shakespeare wrote: 'And his admired loved darling,' an echo of 'admired Miranda,' 3. 1. 37–8.

106. *the spirit:* F. 'the ſpirits:' which is awkward. Some read 'their' for 'the'; but it is simpler to take it as compositor's grammar and leave out the *s*.

4. 1.

3. *third* Many emend 'thrid' or 'thread,' unnecessarily. The other 'thirds' were Prospero himself and his wife; but his wife is dead and so Miranda is now 'that for which he lives.'

9. *hereof* F. 'her of'; compositor's misdivision of Shakespearian spelling 'herof' (cf. 'her's' for 'here's,' *Lear*, 3. 4. 39). 'Hereof' refers to 'rich gift.' F2, which most edd. follow, reads 'boast her off'; but 'boast off' =

(conjecturally) 'cry up' has no parallel to support it;
cf. note l. 74.

13. *gift* (Rowe) F. 'gueſt,' misprint for 'guift.'

17. *rite* F. 'right' v. note l. 96.

23. *lamp* (Elze) F. 'lamps' cf. 'Hymen's torch,' l. 97.

THE MASQUE. v. pp. 80–1. The punctuation of
the Masque-verse is noticeably less careful than that of
the rest of the play, and we have found it necessary to
depart from it here and there.

64. *pionéd and twilléd* A vexed passage. The agri-
cultural interpretation (v. G.) seems the most satisfactory.

74. *her* (Rowe) F. 'here' cf. note l. 9. F. reads S.D.
'Juno descends' here, which mod. edd. omit. But 'her
peacocks, etc.' supports F. reading. Juno's car was evidently let down slowly from above at this point; she has
alighted by l. 100.

84. *A contract of true love to celebrate*, cf. l. 132 'and
help to celebrate/A contract of true love'—practically
word for word repetition.

85. *donation* W. J. Lawrence (v. p. 81 n.) plausibly
suggests that at the Court performance of 1612–13 the
goddesses made an actual 'donation' of some kind to
the betrothed royalties present and that Juno's words
'go with me,' etc. (l. 103) were the signal for the
players to approach the Princess and her Elector with
their gift. If so, the song was doubtless sung during
this presentation.

90. *scandalled*, i.e. brought into disrepute (cf. *Cor.*
3. 1. 44) or possibly an obsolete spelling of 'sandalled';
cf. 'scilens' for 'silence' 2 *Hen. IV*, 5. 3. 1, etc.

96. *bed-rite* (Steevens) F. 'bed-right' The two spellings were interchangeable at this period, cf. note l. 17.

99. *Her son...waspish-headed arrows*, (Maunde
Thompson: privately). F. 'Her waſpiſh headed ſonne
has broke his arrowes.' The arrows of Cupid have stings
in their heads. The compositor has transposed the epithet.

106. *marriage-blessing* (Warburton)   F. 'marriage, blessing'

110. *Ceres* (Theobald)   F. gives whole song to Juno. *Earth's increase* (Aldis Wright) F. 'Earth's increaſe' F2. 'Earth's increaſe and'

114–15. *Spring come* etc. v. p. 80.

123. *a wondred father and a wise* 'Wondred' with a side-reference to Miranda, the 'wonder.' 'Wise' printed 'wife' in some copies of F. but 'wise' seems more probable. The whole may be interpreted as a compliment to King James.

124–25. *Sweet now* etc. F. gives this to Prospero, but he can hardly address Ferdinand as 'sweet.' Aldis Wright first suggested that the words belong to Miranda.

128. *windring* Either 'wandring' or 'winding' are possible.

146–47. *You do look* etc. Aldis Wright comments on l. 146: 'This line can scarcely have come from Shakespeare's pen. Perhaps the writer who composed the Masque was allowed to join it, as best he might, to Shakespeare's words, which recommence at "Our revels now are ended."' The criticism is suggested by the halting metre, but the sense of ll. 146–47 is equally clumsy. It is Prospero and not Ferdinand who looks 'dismayed' and needs the encouragement 'Be cheerful, sir.' v. p. 82.

164. *I think thee, Ariel:* F. 'I thank thee Ariel:' which is surely pointless. The context cries out for 'think'; and 'thank' is a minim-misprint (T.I. p. xli). It is not necessary to alter the number of strokes, since 'thinck' is a Shakespearian spelling.

165. F. prints 'Spirit' with l. 166.

167. *when I presented Ceres,* i.e. Ariel had played Ceres in the Masque, v. p. 81.

169. broken line.

170–71. *Say again* and *I told you* suggest that Prospero has already heard of Ariel's doings with the 'varlets,' and that the relevant passage has been 'cut.'

184. *O'er-stunk their feet.* Their feet, being at the bottom of the pool, could hardly be offensive. We should probably read *sweat* for 'feet.' The Shakespearian spelling is 'swet' (e.g. *Lucr.* 396); and a comparison of 'sword' in l. 8 with 'feet' in l. 16 of the Facs. will show how 'swet' could be mistaken for 'feet,' if the initial stroke of the *w* were begun too close to the *s*.

193. *them on* (Rowe) F. 'on them'

194–95. *Pray you, tread softly* etc. Printed as prose in F.

222–23. *King Stephano.* Trinculo is thinking of the ballad of 'The old cloak' quoted in *Oth.* 2. 3. 92–99, and containing the lines—

> King Stephen was a worthy peere,
> His breeches cost him but a crowne....

232. *Let's all on* F. 'let's alone' Most edd. read 'let's along,' which lacks palaeographical support. 'One' and 'on' are constantly confused in the Qq, and Shakespeare probably spelt both as 'on.' This marks the misprint as one of misdivision. Cf. *Rom.* 1. 4. 2, 'Or shall we on without apology,' and *M.W.W.* 2. 2. 176.

237–38. *under the line* v. G. 'line', and M. P. Tilley in *Studies in Philology*, July 1924.

240. *Do, do!*=go on! go it! Cf. O.E.D. 'do, 32' and *Troil.* 2. 1. 45, 'Ay, do, do; thou sodden-witted lord.'

256–57. *Mountain...Silver.* There is an obscure mention of 'silver, hill and mountain' in *Die Schöne Sidea* (v. Variorum *Tempest*, p. 339, l. 4) which may refer to spirits. v. pp. xlix, 79.

264. *Lie* (Rowe) F. 'Lies'

5. 1.

2. *My charms crack not:* v. G. 'crack.'

2–3. *Time goes upright with his carriage.* If Prospero were looking at his watch, the position of the hands at

6 o'clock would explain the passage; but his question in the next line makes this interpretation difficult, though note that he and Ariel check the time by each other at 1. 2. 239. Perhaps he means simply: I have almost finished my task, and Time's burden is therefore light.

16. *run* F. 'runs'

41. *masters* Hanmer read 'ministers,' which is a better reading, and if written with a minim short might easily have been mistaken for 'maisters.'

43. *azured* A common form of 'azure' in the 16th and 17th cents.; v. N.E.D.

60. *Now useless boil* etc., i.e. Alonso's brain is but a tumour. F. '(Now vſeleſſe) boile' Probably Shakespeare intended the second bracket to follow 'skull,' but forgot to insert it, as happens occasionally in other texts. Most mod. edd. read 'boiled,' which is ugly, and quote *Wint.* 3. 3. 64, which is pointless, since there 'boiledbrains' = hot-headed youths—quite a different thing. It would improve matters, perhaps, if we read 'brain' for 'brains' in l. 59.

61. This broken line is too effective not to be intentional.

63. *e'en* F. 'ev'n,' an unusual contraction, and possibly a misprint for 'eũ,' i.e. 'ever' which would give better sense.

75. *entertained* (F2) F. 'entertaine' *e:d* misprint (cf. note 1. 2. 155).

76. *who* (Rowe) F. 'whom'; compositor's grammar.

81–2. *shores...lie* (Malone) F. 'shore...ly'; compositor's grammar.

95. F. divides 'miſſe/Thee'

130. *No...* v. p. 85.

133. *faults* (F4) F. 'fault'; compositor's grammar.

137. *who* (F2) F. 'whom' N.B. These slips increase as the play draws near an end.

146–47. *and súpportable* etc. Capell jestingly remarks that 'súpportable' is insupportable. Perhaps the solution is to divide that word, retain the F. 'deere' for 'dear,' and read 'less' for 'loss' (an *e:o* misprint, induced by the hypnotic influence of 'loss' thrice repeated in the preceding lines). 'Dere' or 'deere' = pain, injury, v. N.E.D., which quotes Chaucer, Malory, Chapman, etc. This would give us—

> As great to me as late, and support, able
> To make the dere less, have I means...

i.e. Prospero says in effect: 'I have means of support weaker than yours to comfort my sad heart; for I have lost my daughter—the only woman left to me.'

157. *offices of truth...These words* F. 'offices of truth: Their words' Capell read 'these' for 'their,' but most edd. read 'their' and alter the F. colon into a comma to make sense. The F. colon and capital T, however, are worthy of every respect, and make 'their' impossible. 'Theise' or 'theis,' a common 16th century spelling for 'these' which Shakespeare uses in F. *Hen. V*, 3. 2. 122, and three times in the *More* Addition, might easily be read as 'their,' if it lacked the final *e*. Note too the hypnotic effect of '*their* reason' and '*their* eyes.'

175. *Yet* (Moore Smith, *Mod. Lang. Rev.* XI. 99). F. 'Yes' The emendation seems self-evident. Final *s* is several times confused with *t* in the Qq.

200. *remembrance* (Rowe) F. 'remembrances'; compositor's grammar. Some read 'remembrance'' to indicate silent *s* after *c*-sound; but Shakespeare did not write for the *eye*.

220. *overboard* F. 'ore-boord'

223. *the next,* F. 'The next:'

228. *events* Some copies F. 'evens'

231. *of sleep* Edd. interpret 'from sleep'; but Pope read 'asleep,' which is quite possible, the compositor incorrectly expanding 'a' to 'of,' as happens in other texts; cf. *M.N.D.* 3. 1. 84.

237. *her trim* (Theobald) F. 'our trim'

249. *Which shall be shortly single*, i.e. my leisure will soon be unbroken, absolute. F. '(Which ſhall be ſhortly ſingle).' Cf. *Mac.* 1. 3. 140, 'my single state of man.' Most edd. read 'which shall be shortly, single I'll resolve you', etc.

258. *coragio*, i.e. 'courage!' F. misprints the second 'coragio' as 'Coraſio.'

272. *without her power*. Ambiguous; either 'without her authority' or 'beyond her sphere of influence.'

284–85. *I shall not fear fly-blowing*. Pickling preserves meat from fly-blowing (Steevens).

286. *Why* Some copies F. read 'Who'

290. *sore* v. G.

291. *This is as strange a thing* (Capell) F. 'This is a ſtrange thing'

Epilogue. Possibly an apology to James I, author of *Dæmonologie*, for dabbling in magic.

THE STAGE-HISTORY OF
THE TEMPEST

Peter Cunningham (*Extracts from the Accounts of the Revels at Court*, 1842, p. 210) published the following entry, which he professed to have discovered in the Revels Accounts for the year 1611:

> By the Kings Players: Hallomas nyght was presented att Whithall before ye kings ma^tie A play called the Tempest.

This entry was long suspected or declared a forgery; but its genuineness has been recently affirmed by Mr Ernest Law (*Some Supposed Shakespeare Forgeries*, 1911); and, if Mr Law's arguments stand the test of further critical exploration of the problem, the entry may be regarded as the earliest record of a performance of *The Tempest*. There is some reason for believing that the performance at Court had been preceded by one or more public performances at the Blackfriars play-house. Malone states, on the authority of the Vertue MSS, that the play was acted by the King's Company before Prince Charles, the Princess Elizabeth and the Elector Palatine, in the beginning of the year 1613. In the preface (dated December 1, 1669) to *The Tempest, or The Enchanted Island*, Dryden states that 'the play itself had formerly been acted with success in the Black-Fryers.'

The subsequent stage-history of *The Tempest* is almost entirely a tale of distortion and misuse. *The Tempest, or The Enchanted Island* (published in 1670) was a version of the play made by William D'Avenant, with some help from Dryden (*Cambridge History of English Literature*, VIII. 28, 398). Between them, they achieved what was doubtless considered to be artistic symmetry, by giving to Miranda a younger sister, Dorinda, and a male counterpart in Hippolyto, a youth who had never seen a woman;

to Caliban a female monster, Sycorax, and to Ariel a female sprite, Milcha. The first performance of this play, which took place at the Duke's Theatre, Lincoln's Inn Fields, on November 7, 1667, was attended by Samuel Pepys, who liked it so well, and especially 'a curious piece of musique in an echo of half sentences,' in a duet between Ferdinand and Ariel (the music was by John Banister and Pelham Humphrey), that he visited it at least six times more, the last occasion that he records being on January 21, 1669. In 1674 this version, altered and turned into an 'opera' by Shadwell, with music by Locke and others, was produced at the Dorset Gardens Theatre. There is no evidence to show whether *The Tempest* performed at Lincoln's Inn Fields on October 13, 1702, was Shakespeare's or D'Avenant and Dryden's. The lists of characters given in Genest's *Account of the English Stage* show that D'Avenant and Dryden's version, with or without alteration, was that produced at Drury Lane on June 4, 1714, January 2, 1729, and (by Garrick) on December 26, 1747. On January 31 and May 19, 1746, however, Shakespeare's play was acted there. The return to Shakespeare was not to persist, for on February 11, 1756, 'a new opera, called *The Tempest*, altered from Shakespeare,' with music by John Christopher Smith, was produced at Drury Lane by Garrick, who was suspected of having compiled the book. His production at Drury Lane, on October 2, 1757, appears to have been Shakespeare's play; and so does the first recorded production of *The Tempest* at Covent Garden, which took place on December 27, 1776. The representations at Drury Lane on January 4, 1777, and March 7, 1786, were probably an arrangement by Sheridan, with music by Thomas Linley, junior.

On October 13, 1789, John Philip Kemble produced at Drury Lane a version of *The Tempest*, which was substantially D'Avenant and Dryden's, though he restored a good deal of Shakespeare, 'particularly in the comic scenes.' This version was acted there again in 1797 and 1799. At Covent Garden on December 8, 1806, Kemble produced a new version, 'greatly superior to his first,' in which he restored more of the original. Yet this must have been the version which, played at Covent Garden on July 10, 1815, so disgusted Hazlitt that he 'almost came to the resolution of never going to another representation of a play of Shakespeare's as long as we lived; and we certainly did come to this determination, that we never would go *by choice*.' His account, which appeared in *The Examiner* on July 23, 1815 (*Hazlitt*, ed. Waller and Glover, VIII. 234), speaks of 'the common-place, clap-trap sentiments, artificial contrasts of situations and character, and all the heavy tinsel and affected formality which Dryden had borrowed from the French school,' and of the 'anomalous, unmeaning, vulgar, and ridiculous additions,' and dubs the whole representation 'farcical.' Dryden and D'Avenant's version was still the basis of *The Tempest* as acted, with Macready as Prospero, at Covent Garden, on May 15, 1821; additional songs and dialogue and a pantomime show making bad worse; but on October 13, 1838, when Macready was himself manager of Covent Garden, he staged there Shakespeare's play, only slightly altered. Shakespeare's play was acted by Samuel Phelps at Sadler's Wells in 1847 and 1849, and by Charles Kean (who made some alterations in it and gave Ariel's songs to Juno) at the Princess's Theatre in 1857. The play was also produced by Herbert Beerbohm Tree at the Haymarket Theatre in 1904. Tree chose the part of Caliban for himself: in general, Prospero has been considered the principal male part in the play; and Ariel has been a favourite part with actresses and female singers.

HAROLD CHILD.

GLOSSARY

Note. Where a pun or quibble is intended, the meanings are distinguished as (*a*) and (*b*)

ADVANCE, raise, lift up; 1. 2. 413; 4. 1. 177

A-HOLD, a-hauled, i.e. hauled right into the wind so as to re-set canvas; 1. 1. 49

ARGIER, old form of 'Algiers'; 1. 2. 261, 265

ASPERSION, dew, shower; 4. 1. 18

ATTACHED, seized, arrested; 3. 3. 5

AVOID, depart, quit; 4. 1. 142

BARNACLE, a kind of wild goose, formerly believed to be hatched from the fruit of a tree by the sea-shore or from sea-shells ('barnacle-shells') growing on it or on a ship's bottom (O.E.D.); 4. 1. 249

BASS MY TRESPASS, the thunder echoed 'Prosper' like a burden (cf. the 'burthen' to Ariel's song 1. 2. 384); 3. 3. 99

BATE, 'bate me a full year,' remit a year of service. Ariel uses the language of a London apprentice (A. W. Reed; privately); 1. 2. 250

BAT-FOWLING, (*a*) killing birds by holding a lantern close to their roost, beating the bush with bats or sticks, and knocking down the victims as they blunder against the light; (*b*) gulling a simpleton, v. O.E.D. Gonzalo is the 'fowl,' and Sebastian proposes to use the stolen 'moon' as the lantern; 2. 1. 182

BEAK, prow; 1. 2. 196

BERMOOTHES, the Bermudas; 1. 2. 229. On July 29, 1609, the *Sea-Adventure*, one of a fleet carrying colonists to Virginia was wrecked on the Bermudas,

BLUE-EYED = with blue eyelids. A sign of pregnancy (cf. Webster, *Malfi*, 2. 1. 67); 1. 2. 269

BOIL, seethe; 5. 1. 60

BOMBARD, a large leather vessel containing liquor; 2. 2. 22

BOURN, BOUND OF LAND, boundaries, landmarks; 2. 1. 151

BUTT, v. *carcass*; 1. 2. 146

CANDIED, frozen; 2. 1. 276

CAPABLE OF, impressionable to; 1. 2. 354

CARCASS OF A BUTT, i.e. a leaky old tub of a vessel; 1. 2. 146

CAT O' MOUNTAIN, wild cat; 4. 1. 262

CHEEK, 'to th' welkin's cheek'; 1. 2. 4. (*a*) Cf. *Ric. II.* 3. 3. 57 'the cloudy cheeks of heaven'; (*b*) Miranda is also thinking of 'cheek' = the side of a grate; v. O.E.D. 'cheek' sb. 14 and *Oth.* 4. 2. 74: 'I should make very forges of my cheeks, That would to cinders burn.' Hence 'dashes the fire out' and 'stinking pitch'

CHEERLY, blithely; 1. 1. 5

CHOUGH, jackdaw, chatterer; 2. 1. 263

Coil, tumult, uproar; 1. 2. 207

Content, desire; 2. 1. 266

Coragio! i.e. courage!; 5. 1. 258

Corollary, supernumerary; 4. 1. 57

Courses, the two small sails attached to the lower yards of a ship (O.E.D. 32); cf. *try with main course*; 1. 1. 35

Cout, colt, befool; 3. 2. 120

Crack, 'My charms crack not.' His project 'gathers to a head' like an ulcer, ready to 'crack'; 5. 1. 2

Cramps, rheumatic pains such as attack old people; 1. 2. 326, 370; 4. 1. 261; 5. 1. 288

Crisp, rippled; 4. 1. 130

Deck, the poop-deck in the stern of a vessel; 1. 2. 197

Decked, adorned (as with pearls); 1. 2. 155

Demi-puppets, cf. *drollery*; 5. 1. 36

Discharge, performance; a theatrical term (cf. *M.N.D.* 1. 2. 95); 2. 1. 251

Distinctly, separately; 1. 2. 200

Do! A word of encouragement= go on! (cf. *2 Hen. IV* 2. 1. 58); 4. 1. 240

Dollar, the German thaler. Sebastian takes 'entertainer' as an inn-keeper or performer; 2. 1. 17

Dowle, a filament of a feather; 3. 3. 65

Drollery, puppet-show; 3. 3. 21

Eye, spot of colour; 2. 1. 55

Flat-long, i.e. with the flat of the sword; cf. *Arcadia* 'the pitilesse sworde...did hit flat-long' (Variorum *Tempest*); 2. 1. 178

Flote; 1. 2. 234. Generally, but doubtfully, interpreted as 'sea'; v. O.E.D. 'float' sb. 3. 'Flote,' however, meant commonly 'flotilla' or 'fleet' and was applied particularly to the Spanish fleet; 'upon the Mediterranean flote' may therefore ='making for the Mediterranean flotilla.' Cf. *Cym.* 1. 4. 170 'make your voyage upon her'

Foil, 'put it to the foil'=disgrace it; 3. 1. 46. A wrestling phrase; cf. *Sh. Eng.* ii. 456

Foison, plenty; 2. 1. 162; 4. 1. 110

Foot, 'my foot my tutor!'; 1. 2. 474. The foot is Miranda, daring to instruct the head, Prospero

Forth-rights and meanders, paths straight and winding; 3. 3. 3

Foundered, gone lame; 4. 1. 30

Fowl weather, cf. *bat-fowling*; 2. 1. 141

Fraughting souls, souls forming the ship's freight; 1. 2. 13

Freshes, freshets, streams of fresh water (cf. 'fresh springs,' 1. 2. 339); 3. 2. 66

Frippery, old clothes' shop; 4. 1. 227

Gaberdine, cloak; 2. 2. 40, 114

Gentle and not fearful, i.e. a civilised being, not a savage like Caliban; 1. 2. 473

Gilded, flushed, made drunken; 5. 1. 281. O.E.D. quotes Fletcher, *Chances*, iv. 3 '*Duke.* Is she not drunk too? *Con.* A little gilded o'er'

Glass, hour-glass. 'At least two glasses' (1. 2. 240), i.e. some time between 2 and 3 P.M.

(cf. 'three hours' mentioned by Alonso, 5. 1. 137, 187, and 'three glasses since' by the Boatswain, 5. 1. 224). The whole action of the play covers from three to four hours, between 2 and 6 P.M. (cf. 'on the sixth hour' 5. 1. 4). Some have supposed that Shakespeare erred in making the nautical glass an hour and not a half-hour glass; but v. *Sh. Eng.* i. 163–4

HA? eh? 2. 2. 61

HIGH-DAY, old form of 'hey-day'; 2. 2. 191

HINT, occasion; 1. 2. 134; 2. 1. 3

HOODWINK, cover up; a hawking term; 4. 1. 206

JACK (PLAYED THE), (*a*) knave, (*b*) Jack o' lantern, or will o' the wisp; 4. 1. 197

JUSTIFY, prove; 5. 1. 128

KEEPERS, i.e. guardian angels (cf. *Ham.* 1. 4. 39); 3. 3. 20

KIBE, ulcerated chilblain on the heel; 2. 1. 273

LAUGHTER, a sitting of eggs; 2. 1. 32

LIE DROWNING THE WASHING OF TEN TIDES; 1. 1. 57; i.e. worse than the fate of captured pirates, who were fastened to the shore, near Wapping Old Stairs, at low-water mark, until three tides had passed over them; v. *Sh. Eng.* ii. 156

LINE, lime-tree; 4. 1. 193, 236; 5. 1. 10. 'Under the line'; 4. 1. 237, i.e. at the equator. A quibble upon 'line' (lime-tree). Stephano is still 'red-hot' and now has the jerkin round his waist. 'Lose your hair,' i.e. by fever, in crossing the equator; the jerkin was made of fur. 'Line and level'; 4. 1. 240, (*a*) a carpenter's phrase='exactly'; (*b*) Trinculo may also be quibbling on 'level'=levy, tax. v. O.E.D. 'level'

LIVER, formerly considered the seat of the passions; 4. 1. 56

LOOSE, turn loose (for breeding); 2. 1. 124

LUGGAGE, military luggage, camp-follower's pickings (cf. 1 *Hen. IV*, 5. 4. 160); 4. 1. 232; 5. 1. 300

MAIN-COURSE, mainsail; v. *try*; 1. 1. 35

MANAGE, control. Literally, a rider's control of his horse; 1. 2. 70

MEDDLE WITH, mingle with, engage; 1. 2. 22

MIRACULOUS HARP. Amphion raised the walls of Thebes by music; Gonzalo raises walls and houses too; 2. 1. 85

MOE, more in number. Formerly 'more'='more in quantity' only; 2. 1. 131; 5. 1. 235

MOPING, bewildered; 5. 1. 241

MUSE, marvel at; 3. 3. 36

NATURAL, (*a*) idiot, (*b*) not un-natural; 3. 2. 33

NATURE, natural affection; 5. 1. 76

NERVES, sinews; 1. 2. 489

NINNY, 'pied ninny,' referring to the jester's motley; 3. 2. 62

NOBODY, 'the picture of Nobody'; 3. 2. 125. Probably a reference to the sign of Nobody, used by John Trundle, bookseller and publisher of ballads and broadsides 1603–1626. Cf. Jonson, *Every Man in his Humour*, 1. 3. 58, 'Well, if he read this with patience, I'll be gelt, and troll ballads for Mr John Trundle, yonder, the rest of my morality.' Note the parallel between 'troll ballads' and 'troll the catch' (*Temp.* 3. 2. 116); 'gelt' is perhaps a reference to 'Nobody'

OVER-TOPPING, v. trash; 1. 2. 81
OWE, own; 1. 2. 412, 459; 3. 1. 45

PAIN, labour; 1. 2. 242
PASSION (ob.), grieve; 5. 1. 24
PATCH, fool (derived from the fool's costume); 3. 2. 62
PIONED AND TWILLED; 4. 1. 64, 'pioned' probably=dug and sloped like a glacis; and 'twilled' =plaited like a hurdle (W. F. Dawson, *T.L.S.* 18. ix. 24)
PLANTATION, colonisation. The scoffers quibble on the literal meaning of the word; 2. 1. 142
PLAY THE MEN, i.e. pipe all hands, v. O.E.D. 'play' vb. 29; 1. 1. 10
POCKET UP, conceal. Political slang; Gonzalo was a Councillor; 2.1.67
POLL-CLIPT, pruned; 4. 1. 68
POOR-JOHN, salted hake; 2. 2. 27
PORRIDGE, pease-soup. The mod. sense is post-Sh. Quibble on peace'; 2. 1. 10
PRAISE IN DEPARTING, proverbial expression, i.e. wait till the end before praising; 3. 3. 39
PREMISES, stipulations; 1. 2. 123
PURCHASED, acquired. Legal term; 4. 1. 14
PUTTER-OUT OF FIVE FOR ONE, one who gambles upon the risks of travel; 3. 3. 48; cf. Jonson, *Every Man out of his Humour*, 2.

1, 'I am determined to put forth some five thousand pound, to be paid me five for one, upon the return of myself, my wife and my dog from the Turk's court at Constantinople,' and v. *Sh. Eng.* i. 334

QUAINT, ingenious, clever, dainty; 1. 2. 318; 3. 3. 53 (S.D.)
QUALITY, i.e. Ariel's fellow-spirits. Literally 'profession'; 1. 2. 193

RED-PLAGUE, bubonic plague; note the quibble on 'rid'; 1. 2. 365
RELISH, taste; 5. 1. 23
REMORSE, pity; 5. 1. 76
RID, destroy; 1. 2. 365
ROARERS, roisterers; 1. 1. 16
ROOM, i.e. to tack in; 1. 1. 7
RUN, (*a*) flee in battle; (*b*) make water. Cf. *standard* and note 'lie like dogs,' etc.; 3. 2. 18

SCAMELS=? seamels i.e. gulls; 2. 2. 177
SCANDALLED, infamous; 4. 1. 90
SCREEN; 1. 2. 107, cf. *Mac.* 5. 6. 1, 'Your leavy screens throw down, And show like those you are'
SETEBOS, mentioned in Eden's *History of Travel*, 1577, as a deity or devil of the Patagonians; 1. 2. 374; 5. 1. 262
SHIFT; 5. 1. 257, Stephano, the butler, is perhaps quibbling on the terms of his profession (cf. *Rom.* 1. 5. 2 'shift a trencher')
SIEGE, stool, excrement; 2. 2. 109
SIGNORIES, states of northern Italy; 1. 2. 71
SINGLE (i) poor, weak; (ii) unbroken (OED, 4); 5. 1. 249
SOPHY, Shah of Persia; 3. 2. 5

Sore, severe, harsh; 3. 1. 11. Stephano quibbles on this meaning at 5. 1. 290 'I should have been a sore one'

South-west (blow on ye); 1 2. 324. Cf. *Batman upon Bartholome* (1582): 'Southern winds corrupt and destroy; they heate and maketh men fall into sicknesse'

Stale, decoy; 4. 1. 187

Stand to, fall to; 3. 3. 49

Standard, (*a*) standard-bearer. King Stephano pictures himself at the head of his armies; (*b*) Caliban cannot 'stand' as Trinculo notes; (*c*) a conduit. v. *run*; 3. 2. 16, 17

Stock-fish, dried cod, beaten before boiling; 3. 2. 69

Stomach, courage; 1. 2. 157

Stover, coarse grass; 4. 1. 63

Supplant, root out, pull out; 3. 2. 50

Sustaining garments, i.e. their clothes helped them to float; 1. 2. 218. A strange idea, found again in *Ham.* 4. 7. 176

Tabor, a small drum; 3. 2. 123 (S.D.); 4. 1. 175

Teen, trouble; 1. 2. 64

Tell, count; 2. 1. 15

Temperance, temperature; 2. 1. 42. A puritan name in l. 43, or possibly a reference to the very indelicate 'Temperance' in Chapman's *May Day* (pub. 1611)

Time (in good), indeed! 2. 1. 94

Trash for over-topping, a hunting phrase; 'trash'=check a hound by fastening a weight to its neck; 'over-topping' = out stripping; 1. 2. 81

Treble, make thrice as great; 2. 1. 218

Trick, device; 4. 1. 37

Tricksy, clever, full of devices; 5. 1. 227

Trifle, trick of magic; 5. 1. 112

Try with main-course, i.e. bring the ship close into the wind with only the mainsail set. v. *Sh. Eng.* i. 161–2; 1. 1. 35

Twilled, v. *pioned*; 4. 1. 64

Under the line; 4. 1. 237 v. *line*

Unshrubbed, bare of bush or tree; 4. 1. 81

Unstaunched, not able to contain water; 1. 1. 47

Up-staring, standing on end; 1. 2. 213

Urchins, hedgehogs, or fiends in that form; 1. 2. 327; 2. 2. 5; 'urchin-shows'=apparitions of urchins. The hedgehog was recognised as an emblem of the devil in Shakespeare's day (cf. *M.W.W.* 4. 4. 49 and 'the hedgepig,' *Macb.* 4. 1. 2)

Vast of night, the desolate hours of night when nature sleeps (cf. *Ham.* 1. 2. 198 'the dead waste and middle of the night'); 1. 2. 328

Verdure, freshness, vigour; 1. 2. 87

Virtue, essence; 1. 2. 27

Visitation, affliction; 3. 1. 32

Visitor, i.e. one taking food ('cold porridge') and 'comfort' to those in distress; 2. 1. 11

Waist, midship; 1. 2. 197

Ward, 'come, from thy ward'= come, off thy guard; 1. 2. 476

Wezand, wind-pipe; 3. 2. 90

WHILE-ERE, a while since; 3. 2. 117

WINK, close the eyes; 2. 1. 213; glimpse, 2. 1. 239; sleep, 2. 1. 282

YARE, quick, brisk, ready; 1. 1. 3, 6, 34; 5. 1. 225

ZENITH, i.e. the height of my fortunes. Astrological term, as befits Prospero; 1. 2. 181